THAT MIGHTY HEART

"The river glideth at his own sweet will ...
And all that mighty heart is lying still."
William Wordsworth, *Upon Westminster Bridge*

For Wendy and Richard,
with our thanks.

Also by John Elinger and Katherine Shock

THAT SWEET CITY
Visions of Oxford

www.katherineshockwatercolours.co.uk

THAT MIGHTY HEART
Visions of London

Poems by JOHN ELINGER
Illustrations by KATHERINE SHOCK

SIGNAL BOOKS
Oxford

First published in 2014 by
Signal Books Limited
36 Minster Road
Oxford
OX4 1LY
www.signalbooks.co.uk

A catalogue record for this book is available
from the British Library.

ISBN 978-1-909930-05-6 Paper

Design and production: Baseline Arts Ltd
Cover design: Baseline Arts Ltd
Cover images: Katherine Shock
Illustrations: Katherine Shock
Printed in India

CONTENTS

INTRODUCTION

I. LONDON TODAY

One river links two cities. Host to three
Olympic Games, with four World Heritage
Sites, London also offers four cathedrals,
five palaces, six 'must see' sights – The Tower,
The Abbey, Parliament, St. Paul's,
Buckingham Palace, and Trafalgar Square –
our seven star museums – the BM,
National Gallery, Tate Britain and
Tate Modern, and the three in Kensington –
eight Royal Parks, nine street or covered markets,
a population of ten million people
who live and work here, or who visit London.

London's a seaport – capital of England –
centre of government, finance and culture –
cram-full of traffic, history and peoples;
statues and stories, spectacle and splendour;
gardens and concerts, theatres and churches;
museums, galleries and monuments;
cafes and restaurants, department stores
in busy boulevards, and quiet squares
where you may rest, reflect – and read this book.
Here is a paradise for visitors
and residents – for all who would explore
the sights of London by the River Thames.

LONDON, THE CAPITAL OF THE UNITED KINGDOM and the centre of the Commonwealth of Nations, is the greatest city in the British Isles – and one of the finest cities of the world. It is a seaport in the south-east of England, with a population of almost fourteen million within the London Metropolitan Area, the largest in the European Union. London is formed of concentric circles, while appearing almost boundless at the perimeter. The largest ring is the metropolitan region (population about 21 million), within which nestle the metropolitan area (fourteen million), and the Greater London Urban Area (ten million). This book focuses on an inner ring bounded by London's river and canals.

Located in the flood-plain of the lower Thames valley, where the river is tidal, and surrounded by ranges of low hills on three sides, little of London rises more than four hundred feet above sea-level – and much of it lies only a few feet above the high tide mark. The Thames Barrier at Woolwich is designed to protect the city from tidal surges, but will probably need to be strengthened and extended within the next half-century or so. The extensive embankment of the Thames – and the fact that many of its local tributaries now run underground – has transformed London since the early period when it partly consisted of a group of shallow islands in marshland, as names like Chelsea and Battersea reveal.

The climate is temperate, the weather variable, with temperatures rarely falling below −4°C in winter – or rising much above the summer average of 24°C, though the 'ant-hill' effect of a large urban population tends to make the centre of London warmer than its outskirts. During the summer expect some rain at least once a week on average.

London is, in fact, a fusion of two cities, the old Roman City of London and the later Saxon City of Westminster. These combined to create modern London, which has spread in all directions to form the London Metropolitan Area, extending across more than 3,000 square miles with a population density of almost 4,000 per square mile. It is surrounded by a Green Belt, itself under threat from the apparently unstoppable expansion. London, the seat of the national government, is governed by the Greater London Authority – the Mayor and the London Assembly – and the Councils of the 32 London Boroughs, together with the City of London Corporation.

The population is cosmopolitan and includes a diverse range of ethnic groups and cultures speaking more than three hundred languages. Roughly sixty per cent of Londoners see themselves as White, twenty per cent Asian, fifteen per cent Black, with five per cent of mixed race. Almost a third of London's population was born abroad. Some fifty per cent describe themselves as Christian, thirty per cent have no religion (or do not report one), twelve per cent are Muslim, five per cent Hindu and two per cent Jewish.

London is a global city, with particular strengths in the fields of the visual and performing arts, commerce and trade, education and training, entertainment of every kind, fashion, finance, healthcare, the print and broadcast media, professional services, research and development, tourism and all forms of transport.

Almost thirty per cent of the UK's Gross Domestic Product is generated in the London Metropolitan Area. It is one of the world's leading centres of both finance and culture. With forty or more universities and university colleges, it has the greatest concentration of higher education in Europe – and more than 400,000 enrolled students. After finance, the largest business sectors are the media, professional services and retail. More than 85 per cent per cent of the workforce is found in the service industries.

London's transport systems include roads, railways, river and air transport. It is advisable to use public transport for road journeys in the central area. the average speed of a private car in the rush hour is about ten mph. The bus network is extensive and effective, providing over six million passenger journeys each weekday. Look for the iconic red double-deckers, which alongside the black cabs and the tube network, are the most popular means of travel within London. The London Underground is the oldest metro-system in the world, but is being extensively modernised, and serves London well: it provides over three million passenger journeys each weekday.

The city is the hub of the UK's railway system, with no fewer than eighteen terminal stations, connecting to all parts of Britain – and also (via the Channel Tunnel) to Lille, Paris and Brussels and the whole of continental Europe – and Asia. Once the largest in the world, the Port of London is now only the second largest port in the UK, but it still handles over 45 million tons of cargo each year. The Thames is a significant transport route, with ferries and commuter and tourist boat services in the central area. London boasts the world's largest city airport system, with eight airports, of which the most important are Heathrow and Gatwick.

London is literally a Monopoly board of famous places: Whitechapel and Whitehall, Bow Street and Fleet Street, Leicester Square and Oxford Street, Park Lane and Mayfair. Its annual calendar is crammed with memorable events – from the fireworks over the Thames at New Year to the Christmas celebrations in Trafalgar Square: the Boat Race, the London Marathon, the Lord Mayor's Procession, Trooping the Colour on the Queen's Birthday, the FA Cup Final, Remembrance Day... It is the first city to have hosted the modern summer Olympic Games thrice (in 1908, 1948, and 2012).

With over fourteen million visitors from overseas each year, London is the most visited city in the world. Tourism is one of its major industries, earning an annual income of about £15 billion. The visitors come to admire the buildings and enjoy the parks and squares, learn about London's remarkable history – Dick Whittington, Sherlock Holmes and Jack the Ripper – share its culture and entertainments – Madame Tussauds, the London Aquarium and the new cable car (the Emirates Airline) in Greenwich – explore the cafés and restaurants, indulge in retail therapy and see the sights presented here. They will not be disappointed. London is a place that should be found on everyone's bucket-list – once seen, never forgotten. And a single visit will not suffice! We love it – and hope that you will come to love it too.

2. THE HISTORY OF LONDON

The name of London's Celtic, like the Thames:
no more is known, before the Romans come.
Two thousand years, it has survived –
can it survive a third millennium?

One thousand years ago, a Danish king,
Canute, besieged the City from the Thames,
cutting a channel past old London's bridge.
He gained the crown by such bold stratagems.

But even he could not hold back the sea,
nor turn the tide of national dissent.
Like ours, his disunited kingdom chose
protest in preference to good government.

I wonder what he would have thought today
to see the Barrier designed to halt
the ever-rising tide at Greenwich, and
preserve the City from the flood's assault?

But in the past it wasn't flood, as much
as fire, which threatened to destroy the town.
Its children chanted, 'London's burning!' – for
it seemed more likely it would burn, than drown.

The fires of London number four: the first,
two thousand years ago, when, breaking free,
Queen Boadicea burnt the City in
revenge for Roman rape and perfidy.

The second (by mistake) when spreading fire,
nine centuries ago, consumed St. Paul's
and half the City. Once it had died down,
old London was rebuilt within the walls.

The third fire was the greatest fire
of London, which destroyed in three grim days
of 1666 four hundred streets,
before a change of wind controlled the blaze.

The fourth was Hitler's Blitz, an act of war
as wicked as it proved unwise. We learnt
the virtues of determination, self-
belief, resilience – while London burnt.

The next time – and the last – the City may
not die by fire, but perish in a flood,
when massive tides could inundate the land
round London, and reduce it all to mud.

Look east: the rising sun, and rising sea,
predict the day when London might be gone –
with all its treasures, glory, grandeur – like
the Cities of the Plain, and Babylon.

Follow the river as it flows away
past Greenwich, Gravesend, to the open sea,
where Sheerness and the Maplin Sands reveal
the lonely desolation that may be.

THE HISTORY OF LONDON IS A DRAMA IN FIVE ACTS – separated by even more dramatic conflagrations which almost destroyed the city, but also cleared the way for reconstruction: Boadicea's fire in 61 AD, the accidental fire of 1087, the Great Fire of 1666 (another accident) and Hitler's Blitz – 'the second great fire of London' – in 1940. The intervals between these disasters reduce over time: the trend suggests that the next destruction of London is to be expected around the year 2100, as the poem implies.

Nothing certain is known of London before the Roman invasion in 43 AD. Caesar must have crossed the Thames nearly a century earlier, but he does not mention it. The name is almost certainly Celtic, though the etymology of London is disputed. Archaeology has unearthed evidence of earlier British settlements in the area and possible remains of a wooden bridge. Its strategic importance makes it unlikely that the site of London was completely deserted before the Romans came.

They probably bridged the Thames – and certainly created a military camp, which developed into a fortress, and then a fortified town. This first Roman settlement was destroyed and burnt by Boadicea, Queen of the Iceni, in revenge for Roman atrocities visited upon her family and people. This marked the end of the brief first act of the drama.

The second incarnation of London was more successful. An important walled township gradually developed on the site of the earlier fortress – and of the modern City. It was called Augusta, but the old name re-emerged before long. By the second century AD, London boasted a population of about 60,000. Roman London survives today in the remains of the wall, the excavated temple of Mithras, a Roman galley found in the Thames near Westminster Bridge and the evidence of a carefully planned layout of streets and squares around a central forum. But all the buildings perished in later fires.

Roman London declined after the year 200. By 410 the emperor was forced to recall the legions to Rome, and the Dark Ages began. London itself was almost abandoned. When the Anglo-Saxon invasion began later in the fifth century, the new settlers created a town they called *Lundunwich* (like Greenwich or Woolwich) in the region of modern Westminster to the west of the deserted Roman city. By the end of the seventh century

London had revived to become a major port. But like so much of the country, it declined again in the face of repeated Viking raids and invasions.

Alfred the Great, the first king of a united England, re-founded London in the year 886. The focus of the settlement moved back to the Roman walled city. London gradually grew in size and importance over the next sixty years – and then it suddenly blossomed into the largest town in England by the time of the Conquest, when it came to replace Winchester as the *de facto* capital.

Danish invasions continued during this period; London proved an attractive target for the long-ships. But the city held out against repeated attacks and sieges on land and water until Canute found a way to cut a channel around the southern end of London's bridge and impose a successful blockade. England finally submitted to the Danish king in 1016.

The struggle for supremacy continued for a troubled half-century, until it was dramatically concluded by the Norman invasion and the ascent of William I to the throne. Nothing was ever quite the same again: England – and London – were transformed. They emerged from defeat with new forms of government, new expressions of culture, new social institutions and a new architecture. The English language survived – but in a new form, heavily modified by French and Norse.

William's coronation took place on Christmas Day 1066 in Westminster Abbey, which had been rebuilt by King Edward the Confessor. William built the Tower of London, the first of many Norman castles designed to intimidate the natives. He gave London its own Charter of self-government, and his son began the construction of Westminster Hall beside the Abbey, the forerunner of the Palace of Westminster and our Parliament. The second great fire, which destroyed St. Paul's and much of the City in 1087, only temporarily interrupted – and may have assisted – this great programme of reconstruction and redevelopment. Disasters are sometimes blessings in disguise.

So ends the second act of the drama of London. In the twelfth century it became established as the undisputed capital of England, the seat of government, the location of the royal court and treasury, attracting a population which rose from some 18,000 in 1100 to almost 100,000 by 1300. Henry I granted a Charter of Liberties to the citizens, who asserted their rights to choose a new monarch in 1135 by refusing to recognise his daughter, Matilda, in favour of Stephen, a grandson of William I. The authority of the Lord Mayor of London, earlier the *Port-Reeve,* and of the Corporation was firmly established before the end of the century, and the livery companies and guilds began to be formed.

London was a city of merchants and churchmen, as Chaucer's pilgrims demonstrate. The Port of London was extended along both sides of the river; a new London Bridge was built – which lasted until 1832; the famous skyline, visible in the old prints of medieval London, was dominated by the spire of St. Paul's rising 520 feet towards heaven. Alongside the palaces and government buildings, priories and convents crowded together – Whitefriars, Greyfriars and Blackfriars (the name survives in a bridge and railway station), Benedictines, Carthusians and Austin Friars. With hindsight, the Dissolution of the Monasteries seems inevitable. I wonder whether the universities will suffer the same fate one day.

In the fourteenth century the Black Death struck London and carried off almost a third of the population. The Peasants' Revolt, led by Wat Tyler in 1381, was seen off by the citizens, who remained loyal to the king, Richard II. They similarly helped to defeat the rebellions of Jack Cade in 1450 and Sir Thomas Wyatt in 1554. London could make, or break, those who sought power.

Modern London, like modern England, begins with the advent of the Tudors. Secular power took control of religion, reason displaced faith, trade and commerce prospered. The population increased five-fold during the sixteenth century to reach an estimated 225,000 in 1605. This was the age of Shakespeare and the flowering of the Elizabethan theatres. James I was responsible for the creation of the New River Company, which provided London with a supply of pure water – for a time.

[13]

But these advances came at a high cost. The uncertainty about the succession to Henry VIII and his English Reformation resulted in a grim harvest of martyrdom, political and religious, Protestant and Catholic, including Sir Thomas More, Queen Anne Boleyn, Queen Catherine Howard, Lady Jane Grey, and the Earl of Essex. While the spoils of the dissolved monasteries were distributed among the aristocracy and the livery companies, the beggars and cripples who had depended on them now crowded the streets of London desperately seeking to survive.

Rebellion was a constant threat. In 1605 the Gunpowder Plot intended to cause the death of the King and the destruction of Parliament, but was foiled at the last minute. 'Remember, remember, the fifth of November: gunpowder, treason and plot!' The English Civil War (1642-51) began and ended at Westminster, where Charles I unsuccessfully attempted to arrest five Members of Parliament at the outset, and was tried and executed at its conclusion.

In London the Four Horsemen of the Apocalypse are never far away: Famine, Pestilence, Destruction and Death. Plague had broken out from time to time in the seventeenth century: indeed, there had been a so-called 'Great Plague' in 1625. But the historic Great Plague struck the city in 1665, killing almost 100,000 people or one-fifth of the population. At its height in September, 7,000 deaths occurred in one day. The following year brought the Great Fire of London.

It started in Pudding Lane near London Bridge in a baker's shop on 2 September, 1666. His maid was the first victim. It spread slowly, but gradually took hold of the City. Fanned by a strong wind, it blazed for three days, destroying 89 churches, 400 streets, and more than 13,000 dwellings. Among the notable buildings consumed or damaged by fire were the Royal Exchange, Guildhall and St. Paul's Cathedral. After three days the wind dropped. The fire was brought under control the next day, not least through the calm leadership of King Charles II, who 'kept his head, when all about were losing theirs'. The third act of the drama of London closed amid the smoking ruins.

Once again, London faced the challenge of reconstruction and revival. Work started immediately but it was almost half a century before the new Cathedral of St. Paul's was completed in 1710, during the reign of Queen Anne. This was the age of Dr. Samuel Johnson, George Frederick Handel – and Sir Christopher Wren, who was responsible for the restoration and rebuilding of 51 churches in the City. If you seek his monument, look around you.

The Port of London gradually expanded downstream to the east: the Court and fashionable classes moved westwards towards Whitehall and into new developments like Mayfair. George III acquired Buckingham Palace in 1761. More bridges across the Thames were built and south London began to grow. Georgian architecture made its appearance – but its merits remained unrecognised until the twentieth century. The iron law of taste decrees that aesthetic appreciation lags about a hundred years behind artistic innovation.

London was dirty, dangerous and smelly. The Gordon Riots of 1780 were the most serious uprising seen in London in the eighteenth century, requiring the army to take control of the situation. Crime was a commonplace: there was no police force until the Bow Street Runners were established in 1750. The punishment of crime was severe: more than 200 offences carried the death penalty and transportation to the colonies was a grim alternative. Some three-quarters of the children born in London died before the age of five.

Transport was by river, or on horseback, or in carriages and sedan chairs. Coffee houses became popular – as they are again today. Newspapers began to appear. Modern London started to emerge: it was the place to be. 'You find no man, at all intellectual, who is willing to leave London', said Dr. Johnson. 'No Sir, when a man is tired of London, he is tired of life; for there is in London all that life can afford.'

The Victorian Age transformed London once more. The dangerous, overcrowded and insanitary city became the modern European capital it is today, with wide streets and spacious squares, efficient and effective public transport, a modern police force, new schools and a great University. Clean water and a decent sewerage system improved public health and transformed the Thames from an open sewer into the great river it had once been – and is today. The cholera epidemic of 1848 claimed 14,000 lives; but such episodes became more infrequent as the nineteenth century progressed.

The National Gallery was constructed at the side of the new Trafalgar Square from 1832 and Nelson's Column (like the Gallery, much criticised) was erected in its centre between 1840 and 1843. The Crystal Palace was built for the Great Exhibition of 1851. Prince Albert's influence gave us the Royal Albert Hall and the great Kensington museums – and, after his tragic death, the extraordinary Albert Memorial in Kensington Gardens. The modern Olympic Games came to London in 1908. King Edward VIII brought back pomp and ceremony, to the delight of the citizens. London had become the wealthy capital of a great empire.

But even as George V ascended the throne in 1910, the European catastrophe of the First World War was gathering unstoppable momentum. London was altogether unprepared. The Zeppelin air raids began in 1915; anti-aircraft defence was hastily developed. Although London was placed on a war footing, it suffered considerably less in the First World War than in the Second: no more than a thousand bombs fell on the city, and fewer than 700 people died in the raids. The great loss of life was meanwhile happening in the trenches of Belgium and France, and further afield.

A generation later came the Second World War which, by contrast, led to widespread destruction in London (and many other cities). Some 30,000 people died in the air raids, and more than 50,000 were injured. London was the target, first of the bombing raids of 1940-41, and later of the V1 and V2 flying-bomb and rocket attacks of 1944-45, which killed another 9,000 people and injured almost 25,000 more. What was called the Second Great Fire of London occurred at the end of December 1940, when no fewer than 1,500 fires were started in one night. The Blitz, as Londoners called it, marked the end of the fourth act in the dramatic history of London.

At the end of the war a good deal of London had been damaged or destroyed. In the City, little remained between Cheapside and the Barbican. The streets to the north and east of St. Paul's were devastated, as were the areas around Holborn and Fenchurch Street Station, for example, and the docks. Among the major buildings which suffered in the Blitz were Westminster Abbey and the Houses of Parliament, many of the Wren churches in the City and most of the halls of the livery companies. A major programme of restoration and reconstruction started as soon as the war ended in 1945.

But amidst all this re-building and the post-war austerity London quickly regained its place as the nation's centre of celebration. Following the victory parades of 1945, the city hosted the Olympic Games in 1948, created the Festival of Britain, with the Royal Festival Hall and the Skylon (now only a memory) in 1951, and celebrated the Coronation of Queen Elizabeth II in 1953.

[15]

London was changing. The Clean Air Act of 1956 effectively ended the choking smog which had periodically blanketed the city. Large numbers of Commonwealth immigrants settled in London to provide a willing workforce in the hospitals, buses and sanitation services, and made London one of the most ethnically and racially diverse cities in Europe. A new youth culture emerged, and London became the Swinging City in the 1960s.

There were other changes. The population of Greater London declined after the war from a peak of some 8.5 million in 1939 to fewer than 7 million by the 1980s. London became the target of an urban bombing campaign launched by the Provisional IRA. Racial tension and racial inequality came to a head with the Brixton Riots of 1981. The Greater London Council was abolished in 1986, leaving London without any form of central administration until the creation of the Greater London Authority in the year 2000.

Technological innovation always outstrips social reform. The Thames Barrier was built in the 1980s. At the start of the new century, the Millennium Dome, the London Eye and the new Millennium Bridge were created, followed by the Olympic Park in 2012, when London hosted the Summer Olympics for the third time. Crossrail is in the process of construction to make a new rail link beneath the city. The Mayor of London has championed the cause of a new Estuary Airport. Striking new buildings like The Shard pierce the skyline, while extensive redevelopments reclaim desolate areas of London, as may be seen in the Docklands area and Canary Wharf. Once again, the city grows and prospers.

But the old challenges remain to tease us: the provision of efficient and effective urban transport in a crowded metropolis, public health and public education, the reconciliation of the principles of freedom and equality without losing either, the combination of social variety and diversity with the pursuit of a common culture and common standards of citizenship, and the challenge of an aging population. (Perhaps, the solution lies in the old idea of fraternity?) But – beyond all this – there lies the looming threat of rising sea-levels to the east. The fifth act of London's great historical drama is not finished yet – though we do not expect to live to see it!

3. THE CHOICE OF THE SIGHTS

I wonder why they don't teach choice in school?
Choices are promises you freely make –
first, to yourself; then, others. If you break
a promise, or reverse a choice, the rule
requires you to clear up the mess. And you'll
not find that easy! It's a bad mistake
to void a vow, betray a choice. Heart-ache
and headaches follow, and the costs are cruel.

The marriage-vow's a choice. The wedding band
binds both of you. The marriage will be eased
if each of you has chosen to be pleased
with what you've jointly chosen, and rejoice
as well at the inevitable – and
the unintended – consequence of choice.

WHEN WE WERE YOUNG, OUR TEACHERS TOLD US that we must prepare to make three fundamental choices which would determine the course of our lives: our preferred subject of study, our career and our partner for life. But they omitted to teach us how to do it: we had to work that out for ourselves. We understood we would only get one chance of making each choice. Today, it seems that people get two or three opportunities to get it right. But they still make mistakes.

Fortunately, the choice of sights to recommend to the readers of this book is both easier – and less fraught with danger and distress. We have tried to include both old and new: cathedrals, like Westminster Abbey, St. Pancras Station and Wembley Stadium; towers, like the Tower of London, the Monument and The Shard; palaces, like Hampton Court, Buckingham Palace and Harrods, venues, like the Globe Theatre, the Albert Hall and the Royal Festival Hall, parks, like Hampstead Heath, Kew Gardens and the Olympic Park. Nonetheless, we should admit that it is impossible to do justice to the richness of London's visible history. We were spoilt for choice – and could easily have filled a book twice this size. Readers may be wondering: where is the British Library or the Banqueting House, Tate Gallery or Madame Tussauds, the Wallace Collection or Westminster Cathedral? We can only answer: there wasn't room for everything we would have liked to include. Finished poems describing the Old Curiosity Shop (now closed) and Lords Cricket Ground, for example, have had to be set aside.

We have decided to focus on the central area of London, roughly bounded by the Grand Union Canal to the west, the Thames to the south, and the Regent's Canal to the north and east. These navigable waterways provide central London with a kind of grand, decorative moat. We think it would be a delightful project to circumnavigate the capital along this route one day – or, at least, walk the forty (or more) miles of the adjacent towpath.

Within this 'moated' area lies the centre of London. We introduce the reader to a selection of major attractions, conveniently arranged to provide interesting tours of Westminster, Kensington, Bloomsbury, the heart or epicentre of London, the City and Southwark. But many of the locations we treasure inevitably lie beyond this moat – in every direction. So we have added a selection of outlying sights. Every one, and many more besides, are worth a visit, though they may require at least a day to do them justice.

Our choice has been constrained by a number of intersecting, and often conflicting, criteria: that the sight should inspire an interesting poem and a pleasing picture; that the sights chosen should be linked to provide manageable walks; that the most important sights of London should be included; that they should represent something of the history and variety of the city – past and present, land and water, rich and poor, old and new, peace and war, crown and commoner, men and women, natives and migrants, culture and commerce, and so on. In practice, the poem usually came first, so the poet must take primary responsibility for any distressing or controversial inclusion or omission. But we hope that you, too, will come to admire the sights we love.

4. THE POEMS

Across the lawn
two robins gather stalks and grass,
day after day, to make their nest.
I watch them flit and swoop and pass.
Until their young are fledged and flown
            they never rest.

Across the lane
builders extend the house. They labour
month after month. Progress is slow.
I watch them work – and tell our neighbour:
'Before the summer comes along
            they'll never go.'

I cross a line
and start again – seeking perfection,
year after year, of feeling, thought
and words – to find a true reflection:
the craft of verse so long to learn,
            and life so short.

POETRY HAS TWO ASPECTS: FORM AND MEANING. The poems in this collection are, almost without exception, examples of what is called 'formal verse', and they are mostly descriptive of places in London – topographical poetry. As in the poem above, the author – or the author's voice – is often present, and never entirely absent. Descriptive verse, entirely unleavened by comment, humour or judgment, can seem uninspired, or even boring. Attitude adds interest – or, at least, I hope it will!

I have sought to practise and exemplify a wide range of verse-forms: sonnet and sestina, ballade and villanelle, ode and rondeau, rhymed and blank verse, stanzaic and sequential lines, syllabic and (alliterative) stress measured verse, and several others. Those who would like to know more about verse-form are advised to read Stephen Fry's delightful book, *The Ode Less Travelled* (London, 2005), which admirably combines inspiration and information, advice and example, wit and wisdom. I wish I could have written it. Instead, it has been my vade mecum.

Descriptive topographical verse is out of fashion today. But it has a long and honourable history. Earlier ages offer some striking exemplars of the genre, like Goldsmith's *The Deserted Village*, or Pope's *Windsor Forest*, or Johnson's *London*, to look no further than eighteenth-century England. And all of these great poets, of course, were fully conscious of their classical models from Greek and Latin. Like them, I have tried to add some human interest, where appropriate and possible.

Partly because of the debt I owe to this great tradition – but more because I like the challenge – it seemed appropriate to represent modern London in formal verse that (more or less) scans and rhymes. Our book takes its title from Wordsworth's fine sonnet 'Upon Westminster Bridge', a poem offering a snapshot of an earlier London, caught in the first rays of the rising sun, like some beautiful creature awakening from a deep sleep. Was it ever really like that, I wonder? My poems seek to balance London's undeniable beauty and evident ugliness, its truth and lies, virtues and vices, and realise frankly the smelly bed this lovely vision has risen from, and rests in.

Some of the poems, like the ones on the Tabard Inn or the Albert Hall, attempt to reflect the style or shape of the subject. Others, like the (discursive) sestinas or the (elegiac) villanelles, are written in forms that lend themselves to the topic in view. Readers may find that the poems take on a fuller life, if read aloud: but don't do this on public transport!

5. THE PAINTINGS

There is a moment when
the traffic lights glow, soft and vivid – red
and green and amber – in the gathering dusk,
as if they were on fire.

There have been times – a few
since childhood – when plain ordinary things,
a postbox or a coin, shine incandescent
and make me hide my eyes.

Too often do we miss
the miracle of colour in our lives:
each word, each letter – white, black, red or blue –
my rainbow alphabet!

Katherine Shock writes:

THE OPPORTUNITY TO PAINT IN LONDON is one I had long hoped to have, but could never see how it would fit into a busy life based in Oxford. I felt I knew and loved it as my birthplace and origin, but no-one can know London fully. With the arrival of plans for this book came the courage to take on the challenge of painting it. Would I be able to recreate the famous places with a fresh eye, capture the atmosphere and excitement of a London thronging with visitors – and yet which has its unexpected moments of peace and contemplation at the heart of the frantic activity and noise? I was lucky to have the gift of a brilliantly warm summer in 2013 – and the generosity of kind friends, Sue Austin and Nick Lee, who offered me a space in their home whilst I needed it, as well as constant encouragement and enthusiasm.

Often the choice of view depended on the generous shade of one of London's stately plane trees. I had never realised before how refreshing and important they are to relieve the harsh glare of concrete pavements in the sun. I tried to alternate days of working in noise and frenetic surroundings with quiet days in hidden corners. As the paintings piled up, so did my pleasure in this magnificent city – learning constantly of new nooks and crannies or even entirely new areas that I had never ventured into before.

One of the greatest pleasures, however, has been that of meeting so many people who share my love of London. Tourists would stop constantly to enthuse or question or take photos, and I began to feel that I was one of the spectacles of London they had come to enjoy – but it only added to my pleasure. Locals would stroll over to tell me more about a particular area: everyone owns their special places with pride – and wants to share them. Having paints and a pad on your knee is a remarkable way to break down barriers and I can recommend it to anyone.

[23]

6. THE WALKS

Live life as a pilgrimage without an end.
Walk somewhere every day, while you yet can.
Our legs were made for walking. The life-span
proves more rewarding – and it might extend
a few years further – for the ones who spend
some time exploring footpaths. Everyman
found answers, once his pilgrimage began.
And we should follow, when our deaths impend.

Life is a quest without a quarry. We
search for a purpose that is never found.
The end's the journey, not the journey's end.
Our deaths are meaningless: the meaning's bound
up with the living, not the dying. Spend
life freely: only those who live are free.

THERE ARE SIX CONSECUTIVE WALKS IN THIS BOOK, arranged to make one long circular walk through the middle of London. In each case, we have sought to combine views of the natural and built environment with the pleasure of walking beside water. The first walk begins (and the sixth ends) on Westminster Bridge. Each highlights in poetry and illustration seven major sights – though others might have been added, and are identified in the descriptions and maps of the walks. You will find plenty of good opportunities for rest and refreshment, as you explore the city. But take care when crossing roads. Remember (if you are a visitor) that traffic keeps to the left in this country. Use the light-controlled and zebra crossings, wherever possible, for safety's sake. Enjoy the pilgrimage.

With considerable self-constraint, we have allowed ourselves to identify only ten outlying sights beyond the confines of the central area. These could, of course, be reached on foot: indeed the ones along the Thames invite a stroll along the river's towpath (on the southern side). But most readers, we think, will find them by taking taxis, buses or tube-trains. The map on p. shows their locations and nearby underground stations.

[25]

7. AFTERWORD

When my life closes,
what will remain of what I know as me?
Our bodies die, decay, disintegrate.
I like to think these atoms might become
something remarkable – a sunset, water,
or desert roses!

When my life ends,
who will remember what I've tried to be?
Memories die. Words vanish – like a slate
wiped clean. Brave deeds may be recalled for some
few months or years by one or other daughter,
or son, or friends –

and then we're gone.
Nothing at all has immortality.
All sunsets fade. Waters evaporate.
And desert roses wither crumb by crumb.
Though time allows some longer lives, some shorter,
nothing lives on.

IT HAS BEEN A PRIVILEGE AND A PLEASURE for both poet and artist to work together once again to create this book. We have learned a lot since we collaborated a year or two ago to make *That Sweet City, Visions of Oxford* (2013). Both books follow the same general plan, matching the poems and the paintings, arranging them to provide pleasant walks around the two cities, and offering a descriptive and explanatory introduction.

We are once again deeply grateful to James Ferguson, our brave and kind publisher, who believes that readers will wish to buy this book, as they have its Oxford predecessor. We hope he is right. We also wish to thank the designer, Andrew Esson – and Sebastian Ballard, who provided the maps – for all they have done to help us get this far. We have chosen to dedicate the book to our respective spouses, whose comments, corrections, encouragement and patience have been both admirable and exemplary. They know that we can hardly wait to get started on the third volume of the series – once we can agree on the next city of choice!

We also hope that you, gentle readers, will enjoy the book, visit the sights, explore the walks and study our poems and paintings.

[27]

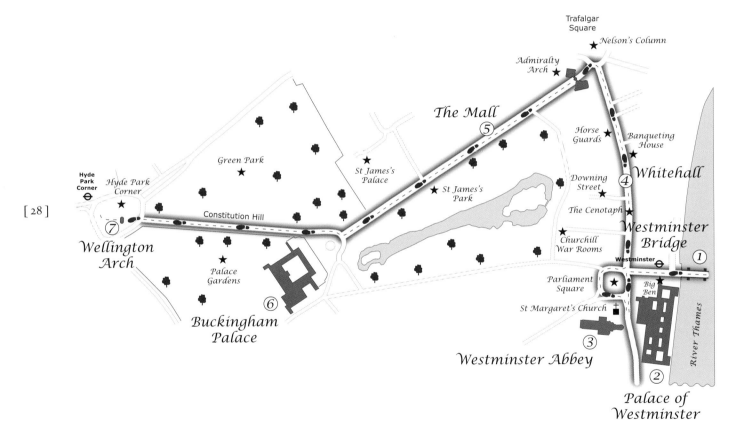

Trafalgar Square

★ Nelson's Column

Admiralty Arch ★

The Mall

⑤

Horse Guards ★   Banbqueting House ★

Whitehall

Downing Street ★

④

The Cenotaph ★

Westminster Bridge

Churchill War Rooms ★

Westminster ⊖

①

Parliament Square

Big Ben ★

St Margaret's Church ✝

River Thames

③

②

Westminster Abbey

Palace of Westminster

Green Park

St James's Palace ★

Hyde Park Corner ⊖

Hyde Park Corner ★

Constitution Hill

St James's Park ★

⑦

Wellington Arch

Palace Gardens ★

⑥

Buckingham Palace

N

0   200
metres

© Mapman.co.uk (2014)

I. WESTMINSTER

The walk begins on westminster bridge, a few yards to the east of Westminster tube station. Lean on the parapet and enjoy the views – both downstream (north) and upstream (south). I imagine that Wordsworth was looking downstream towards the City, when he wrote his great sonnet, but how can we be sure?

Walk back past the Elizabeth Tower with Big Ben telling the hours and turn left into Parliament Square, to find yourself between the palace of westminster (on the left and ahead) and westminster abbey behind St. Margaret's, Westminster, to your right. After visiting the Abbey, cross Parliament Square – and reflect on the lives of those whose statues are found there.

Then walk northwards along Parliament Street and whitehall. Nelson's Column can be seen ahead. On the left, you might visit the Churchill War Rooms, peep into Downing Street, where the Prime Minister and Chancellor live and work, and admire the Horse Guards. The Banqueting House is on the right hand side. You pass the Cenotaph and other notable monuments in the centre of the street.

As you approach Trafalgar Square and Nelson's Column (reserved for a later walk), turn left through the Admiralty Arch into the broad and rose-pink mall. St. James's Park lies to the left; St. James's Palace on the right; buckingham palace is ahead of you.

Now bear right up Constitution Hill, with the Palace Gardens on your left and Green Park on the right-hand side. The wellington arch lies ahead of you, and Hyde Park Corner, where there are buses and a tube-station.

WESTMINSTER BRIDGE

Wordsworth stood here, astonished by this view,
two hundred years ago; but what he saw
was not what we see now. The Thames is more
confined, and less disturbed by traffic; new
buildings replace the city-scape he knew,
and loved; new bridges vault the river for
a population which still seems to soar –
like debt, or drugs; divorce, or drinking, too.

Is our world better now, or worse? The smell
of poverty and sewage gone, the air
is clean. The morning sun's first rays dispel
shadows and sorrow in this City where
we live at peace, in freedom, long, and well.
Perhaps he *was* right: nowhere is more fair.

THE PALACE OF WESTMINSTER

'There are two parts [to a constitution]: first, those which excite and preserve the reverence of the population – the *dignified* parts ... and next, the efficient parts, by which it in fact works and rules.' (Walter Bagehot)

Although this place is seldom dignified,
and often inefficient, liberty
and representative democracy
go hand in hand. Here, parliaments decide
our laws and wars, the tax we must provide,
our public programmes – health, security,
welfare and learning. Here, authority
resides, arousing anger, pain and pride.

Our laws are just; we fight just wars; we pay
our fair share of taxation to endow
good programmes of support for those who may
need help. But, more than this, our laws allow
us all freedom to live our lives: we're free
to speak our minds, dissent, write poetry.

[33]

'How small, of all that human hearts endure,
That part which laws or kings can cause or cure.' (Samuel Johnson)

However good a government may be
the gifts of health, and wealth, and happiness,
are not within its power to grant, unless
to serfs and slaves. Responsibility
for welfare lies with us, the people – free
to learn or not, to earn or not, regress
from, or advance towards, our own success,
and free to live in joy, or misery.

The government determines the conditions
in which we live the lives we choose to live:
in peace or war, security or crime,
with or without a safety net. Its mission's
to set a level playing-field, and give
us all a chance to make good use of time.

[34]

'Unlimited power is apt to corrupt the minds of those who possess it.'
(William Pitt, the Elder)

> Power corrupts – and Parliament holds power.
> Expect a tendency to tyranny,
> to greed and sleaze, amidst the dignity
> of indirect democracy. The Tower
> and Palace of Westminster teach us how a
> good institution's almost bound to be
> infected by the poison which sets free
> corruption – to take root and spread and flower.
>
> Since other forms of government are worse,
> we might despair: but people still can do
> something to hinder the corrupting curse
> of power. The people's saving strength is not
> the power to elect, but rather to
> dismiss, a Parliament that smells of rot.

[35]

WESTMINSTER ABBEY

St. Peter's Church preserves the nation's history.
Here, on St. Edward's throne, monarchs are crowned;
here Cromwell, Lord Protector once, was buried –
and then dug up, and hanged. Our English poets
are remembered here. Kings and queens are married.
This Church King Henry first styled a cathedral.

Then Queen Elizabeth made the cathedral
a 'Royal Peculiar' – bishop-less. Its history,
since the first Henry and Matilda married –
since the first William came here to be crowned –
inspires our great musicians, writers, poets,
whose bodies have been brought here to be buried.

It's here The Unknown Warrior lies buried –
none walk across that grave – in this cathedral
that honours soldiers, scientists and poets
who glorify and celebrate our history –
a Church which Hawksmoor's western towers
      have crowned,
where state solemnity and grace are married.

St. Dunstan gave the Church to monks (unmarried,
poor, and faithful). Another saint is buried
here, Edward the Confessor, who had crowned
his good life by rebuilding the cathedral –
rebuilt again by the third Henry. History
and accident made this a home for poets.

Dan Chaucer was the first of all those poets
memorialised within this Church, who married
the form and meaning, sound and sense, of history
to earn that final honour – to be buried
within their Corner of this royal cathedral,
where queens and kings are wed,
      and monarchs crowned.

The second Queen Elizabeth was crowned
in this great Abbey. Beside the famous poets,
Newton and Darwin lie in the cathedral;
composers – Handel and Purcell – who married
music and words so movingly, are buried
within this storehouse of our nation's history.

A Church where kings and queens are crowned
      and married,
where heroes are remembered, poets buried:
cathedral at the heart of English history.

WHITEHALL

'Of forms of government, let fools contest;
Whate'er is best administered is best.' (Alexander Pope)

Here's the administration: either side
of this great thoroughfare lie offices
for those who serve the public. Policies
and plans Westminster's Parliaments decide
become good practice here. Whitehall's the guide
to governments – it's where our history's
been shaped in peace and war; for this place is
where England's leaders live – and a king died.

The Cenotaph is here: we mark the date
and time of Armistice each year   and will
for years to come – on this spot, where we wait
in silence for those sounds that move me most –
the soldiers, young and old (and time) stand still –
the unresolved cadence of the Last Post.

THE MALL

Past Admiralty Arch you find The Mall,
the *Champs-Elysées* of our Capital.
Here bands play, soldiers march, in celebration
of victories and triumphs of the nation;
and runners in the London Marathon
hang medals round their necks, stick plasters on
their feet, and cool off in St. James's Park –
while vowing never, ever to embark
upon another race! The rose-pink Mall,
with Queen Victoria's Memorial
standing before the Palace at the end,
is where State Visitors pass to attend
a royal banquet with Her Majesty:
a place for crowds and flags and history.

BUCKINGHAM PALACE

This was the Queen's House once, and is the home
of England's Queen today. Built round a square,
Buckingham Palace is a honeycomb
of private rooms and State Apartments, where –

> We serve our gracious Queen.
> Long live our noble Queen!
>   We serve the Queen –
> wish her victorious,
> happy and glorious,
> long to reign over us.
>   We serve the Queen.

State Visitors are entertained, new knights
created, banquets held, awards conferred;
where monarchs grace the nation's solemn rites,
and grant Prime Ministers a private word.

> Dutiful, true and free,
> we serve her faithfully.
>   Long may she reign.
> May she defend our laws
> and ever give us cause
> to sing with heart and voice –
>   long may she reign!

Look at the balcony: the victory
in World War II was celebrated here.
Our King and Queen, their royal family,
waved, as the happy crowds began to cheer.

> When you behold this place,
> symbol of power and grace,
>   bow to our Queen.
> Here she works hard and late;
> here she rewards the great –
> and those who stand and wait.
>   Bow to our Queen!

Here England's history is made and sealed.
Here monarchs wield the power that monarchs
wield.

[43]

THE WELLINGTON ARCH

Here is a hero. This great island has
been conquered three times in its history –
no doubt, in prehistoric ages, as
often: the Celts, for sure, came here across the sea.

But Caesar, Hengist, William – each prevailed.
The Roman, Saxon, Norman Conquests quite
transfigured life in Britain. Others failed:
King Alfred won the victory, when he dared to fight

the Danes; Churchill dispatched the Nazi threat –
another close-run thing – the leader who
promised us blood and tears and toil and sweat;
and Wellington beat Buonaparte at Waterloo.

We honour them, these men who saved the nation –
Alfred and Wellington and Churchill. Though,
I wonder whether greater melioration
comes from defeat, than victory against the foe?

Those Conquests brought us, not just roads and runes
and rhyme, but ended our nostalgic yearning
for the good old ways, old beliefs, old tunes –
in favour of new cultures, languages and learning.

Defeat means transformation, a renewal:
winning means things continue as before.
Gazing upon this arch, I hope that you'll
decide which one today this nation needs the more.

N

0   250
metres

⑦ *Little Venice*

Tow path

★ *Paddington Basin*

Paddington ⊖

Paddington Station ★

Paddington ⊖

London Street

Sussex Gardens

Lancaster Gate

Budge's Walk

Broad Walk

Round Pond ★

Kensington Gardens ★

South Flower Walk

⑥
Kensington Palace

⑤

Albert Memorial

The Serpentine

Hyde Park ★

Park Lane

Albert Gate ★

South Carriage Drive

Hyde Park Corner ⊖

Knightsbridge

★ *Hyde Park Corner*

★ *Harvey Nichols*

Albert Hall

④

Queen's Gate

Imperial College ★

Science Museum

Exhibition Road

Kensington Road

Victoria and Albert Museum

Brompton Road

① *Harrods*

Kensington Museums

③

Natural History Museum

✝ ② *Brompton Oratory*

© Mapman.co.uk (2014)

2. KENSINGTON

THE SECOND WALK STARTS AT HYDE PARK CORNER, where the first one ended. Walk westwards along Knightsbridge, admiring the shops and hotels – or, if you prefer, enter Hyde Park and take the South Carriage Drive to re-enter Knightsbridge through the Albert Gate. As you pass Harvey Nichols, turn half-left into the Brompton Road where you will shortly find HARRODS on your left hand side.

Then continue in a south-westerly direction along the Brompton Road until you come to the BROMPTON ORATORY on the right, followed immediately by the three KENSINGTON MUSEUMS: first the Victoria and Albert Museum, then   in the Cromwell Road – the Natural History Museum, with the Science Museum behind it.

Now turn northwards to walk up Queen's Gate or Exhibition Road. Imperial College and the ROYAL ALBERT HALL lie between them. You are approaching Kensington Gardens. Cross Kensington Road and find the ALBERT MEMORIAL. Then follow the South Flower Walk (west) and the Broad Walk (north) to reach KENSINGTON PALACE.

Leave the Palace behind you and walk north-east past the Round Pond, and along Budge's Walk, through Kensington Gardens to Lancaster Gate. Exit here, and cross the Bayswater Road. Then walk northwards along Lancaster Terrace to join Sussex Gardens. Turn left along London Street, which brings you to Paddington Station; from where you may reach the Paddington Basin and canal by walking through the station towards the underground station on the Hammersmith Line at the north-west end, where you will find signs to the canal. Now follow the towpath in a north-westerly direction to reach LITTLE VENICE. Tube-trains and buses are conveniently located in and near Paddington Station for your return

Harrods

Omnia Omnibus Ubique (Harrods motto)

'All sorts of stuff for anyone, wherever
they may come from' – provided they can pay,
and don't look scruffy! On a single day
300,000 customers endeavour
to find products and services – whatever
they want – food, clothing pets – whatever they
are able to afford – gold, furs ... Some may
frown: Harrods is as popular as ever.

Almost two hundred years of history:
founded in Southwark, moved to Knightsbridge, burnt,
rebuilt, sold and resold and sold again ...
Our greatest store! What Harrods has not learnt
about retail is not worth learning. When
you've time, drop in for shopping, cakes and tea.

THE BROMPTON ORATORY

England's Erastian, subjecting Church to State.
(No Pope's – nor Ayatollah's – jurisdiction here!)
As one, both Crown and Parliament on this are clear:
the Reformation made religion subjugate.

The Brompton Oratory owes fealty to Rome –
and Mary's perfect heart. Italian Renaissance
in style, disciples raised this great Church in response
to Newman's life and lead: his statue here's at home.

Admire the architecture, share the Latin Mass,
enjoy the music from the organ and three choirs.
Elgar was married here. This sacred space inspires
pious respect. Offer a prayer, as you pass.

[50]

Our secular society has little use
for faith. We wonder what the fuss was all about.
Religions have become mere lifestyles. Settled doubt
is epidemic: doubters tolerate all views!

Yet conscience is not dead, although today's zeitgeist
ignores it. Individual conscience never dies.
Lives lived in love and hope and trust may still surprise
us – lives that follow our exemplar, Jesus Christ,

Who made the rules that govern conscience. Conscience is
never self-serving; rarely stands against the laws
of a well-governed nation; if it does, endures
the consequence without complaint, as He bore His.

THE KENSINGTON MUSEUMS

These three museums seem to collect everything! –
fossils and footprints from the start of evolution;
designs and objects which explain the origin
of species, artefacts, ideas ... and pose the question:
is natural selection or intelligence
the shaper of the universe and earthly life?

Museums open minds to other forms of life –
and different modes of thought. Some think
　that everything
was made by God through His divine intelligence:
others believe, with evidence, that evolution
(and physics) give a better answer to the question
of where to find our universe's origin.

The V&A's collection – from the origin
of man's civilisation to our common life
today – of art and artefacts answers the question
of origin decisively: here, everything
has been designed and made by man, not evolution.
This building, with its store, displays intelligence.

In the Science Museum, too, intelligence
is everywhere: Babbage's brain, the origin
of steam and jet engines, the lengthy evolution
of modern medicine, DNA (the source of life),
secrets of time and space and flight – of everything
that helps us find the answer to that basic question.

The Natural History Museum turns the question
another way. The triumph of intelligence
has proved that the whole universe, and everything
within it, is just physics – and the origin
of species, dodos, dinosaurs and human life
lies in the hit-and-miss effects of evolution.

Human intelligence – the hare; and evolution –
the tortoise! Which, I wonder, will prevail?
　The question
is whether in the distant future human life
might yet survive by using that intelligence
to turn back evolution? Not just origin,
but outcome, too – the contest touches everything.

Physics and evolution – or intelligence?
Which answers best the question of the origin
of earthly life, the universe and everything?

The Royal Albert Hall in Kensington
Home to the Proms – Handel's *Messiah* each
Easter – Remembrance   in November – one
Rich treat after another: music, sport and speech,
Operas, ballet, films,   are all found here:
You're looking at   'The Nation's Village Hall',
As it is known to fans   from far and near.
Look at the dome of   moulded iron and glass, which all
Admire; study the frieze   and words above,
Linking the arts and   sciences and toil.
Below, there lies   a legacy of love
Exchanged by Queen and   Prince, devoted, blest and royal –
Royalty's no defence for   broken hearts.
The shape's designed   to be a true ellipse.
Here stands the   Royal Albert Hall of Arts
And Sciences, a hall   no other can eclipse.
Listen to Elgar's *Land of Hope and Glory:*
Learn something more of our unfinished Island Story.

THE
ALBERT
HALL

THE ALBERT MEMORIAL

A nation sorrows, when a Prince is dead:
a widow now, the Queen withdraws, and grieves –
no mourning weeds unworn, no tears unshed.

What might have been, if he had lived instead?
Who looks, his still-born legacy perceives.
A nation sorrows, when a Prince is dead.

Victoria lives on, uncomforted.
No duties now she does, no love receives –
no mourning weeds unworn, no tears unshed.

One chance of peace in Europe forfeited,
(the carnage of a World War none perceives)
a nation sorrows, when a Prince is dead.

Each night retiring to her lonely bed,
a woman time has blest – but time bereaves –
no mourning weeds unworn, no tears unshed.

Her long reign passes: she remains unwed,
alone. This sad Memorial she leaves.
A nation sorrows, when a Prince is dead –
no mourning weeds unworn, no tears unshed.

KENSINGTON PALACE

'An aunt-heap!' cried a king – a commoner
called this palace a children's paradise –
home of queens, some who never were (some were)
some would be: queens in aspic, queens on ice.
Queen Anne, two Marys, dwelt here, Princess Di,
the young Victoria, and Caroline –
some widowed, some in hope, some came to die
(some dead already) in genteel decline.
Ladies in waiting – for a death, or birth,
a husband or a crown – the mundane life
of royalty. Forget the jewels worth
a king's ransom: a queen is still a wife.
Kensington Palace is a bee-hive: queens
live here in honey, would-bes and has-beens.

LITTLE VENICE

I have fallen in love with canal-boat
names: Alpha, Omega, and All That Jazz,
Blue Bird, Blue Swan, Blue Goose, Blue Jay – each has
its charm and grace. I watch the barges float
along the calm canal – Blue Moon, Blue Goat –
thinking of names, like Bedknobs, Bedlam, Baz,
The Bees Knees, serious or comic, as
precious as any child's name I might quote.

This is where I could spend eternity
in peace, watch passing boats and years, the moss
growing, the seasons come and go, and see
boats' names reflecting human loves – My Gal,
Midas, or Mischief. When I die, just toss
my ashes in the Regent's still Canal.

[61]

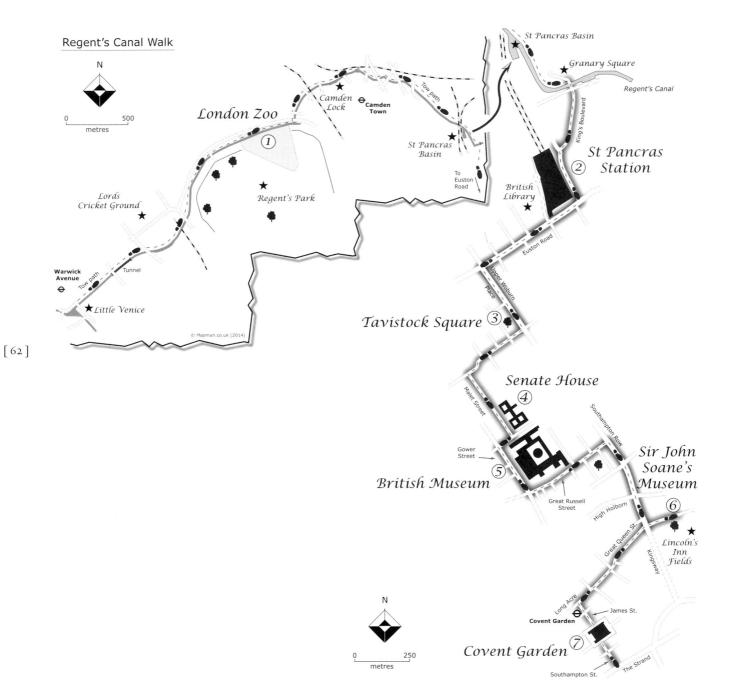

Regent's Canal Walk

N

0   500
metres

London Zoo

①

Camden Lock

Camden Town

St Pancras Basin

Tow path

To Euston Road

St Pancras Basin

Granary Square

Regent's Canal

King's Boulevard

St Pancras Station

②

British Library

Euston Road

Lords Cricket Ground

Regent's Park

Warwick Avenue

Tow path   Tunnel

Little Venice

© Mapman.co.uk (2014)

[62]

Upper Woburn Place

Tavistock Square ③

Senate House ④

Malet Street

Southampton Row

Gower Street ⑤

British Museum

Great Russell Street

High Holborn

Sir John Soane's Museum

⑥

Lincoln's Inn Fields

Great Queen St.

Kingsway

N

0   250
metres

Long Acre   James St.

Covent Garden

Covent Garden ⑦

Southampton St.   The Strand

3. BLOOMSBURY

IF YOU WANT TO COMPLETE THE WHOLE OF OUR CIRCULAR ROUTE through London, you should start the third walk at Little Venice, where the second walk ended. Follow the towpath of the Regent's Canal which branches north-east from the junction. Lords Cricket Ground lies to the left. The canal will lead past Regent's Park and the London Zoo (AN A-Z OF LONDON'S AMAZING ZOO!). Or you might start the third walk at the Zoo, most easily reached by bus.

Then continue eastwards along the canal until you reach the St. Pancras Basin. Continue round a sharp left-hand bend and exit into Granary Square. Cross the bridge and Goods Way to reach King's Boulevard, which takes you to ST. PANCRAS STATION. Walk south-westwards along the Euston Road, past the new British Library, until you come to the left turn into Upper Woburn Place. Take this road southwards to find TAVISTOCK SQUARE on the right-hand side. Leave the Square at the southern corner and walk south-westwards until you reach Malet Street. Turn left to reach THE SENATE HOUSE of the University of London.

Continue down Malet Street; turn right into Montague Place; and then left into Gower Street. The BRITISH MUSEUM is on your left: to reach the entrance, continue along Bloomsbury Street and turn left into Great Russell Street. From here walk further north-westwards along Great Russell Street and Bloomsbury Place to reach Southampton Row, where you should turn right. Continue along Southampton Row and cross High Holborn; then walk down Kingsway to turn left into Remnant Street and reach Lincoln's Inn Fields and SIR JOHN SOANE'S MUSEUM.

Return along Remnant Street, cross Kingsway, and continue south-westwards along Great Queen Street and Long Acre until you reach a left turn into James Street, bringing you into COVENT GARDEN, where there is an underground station nearby, and buses may be found by continuing southwards along Southampton Street to the Strand

AN A-TO-Z OF LONDON'S AMAZING ZOO!

Here are hundreds of species, thousands of creatures, millions of visitors:
aardvarks, ant-eaters, armadillos (and antelope also) adorn any animal alphabet;
butterflies, bats, bears, bison (besides bullfrogs) belong;
cobras, crocodiles, chameleons charm coach-parties;
donkeys, dragons, dingoes delight day-trippers
Enthusiasts eye elephants, eagles – even electric eels! –
find frogs, flamingos, field-mice fascinating.
Gorillas, giraffes, gibbons gambol gracefully –
hedgehogs, hippopotamus, horses – humans – herd here.
(I idolise ibis!)
Jellyfish jostle;
kookaburras kaw;
lions, llamas, lizards laze lethargically;
monkeys, meerkats, macaws, mate, multiply, misbehave ...
Note – newts, nymphs, nightingales!
Observe onlookers oh-ing over oryxes, okapis, ostriches, oxen.
Piranhas, penguins, porcupines please perceptive people.
(Quaggas quaff quietly.)
Rattlesnakes, reindeer, rats run riot!
Sightseers seem spellbound seeing sloths, stingrays, sea-horses ...
... tortoises, tigers, tarantulas!
(Unicorns unfortunately unseen.)
Visitors view vicious vultures, venomous vipers, various voles –
watch in wonder wombats, warthogs, wallabies.
Xanthoura (extinct), Xiphosura (extant), xenopus (exotic), xiphias (excellent) excite excursionists.
Yaks yawn. (You yack!)
Zebras, zebu, zho, zibet, zingel, zizel, zoozoo, zorro ... zillion Zoo-denizens!
An alphabet of animals for zealous zoologists is here.

St. Pancras Station

I love the names of London's railway
stations: Paddington, St. Pancras, Euston,
King's Cross, Charing Cross, Victoria,
Liverpool Street and London Bridge;
Marylebone, Moorgate, Blackfriars,
Cannon Street and Kensington Olympia;
Broad Street, Fenchurch Street and Farringdon;
Holborn Viaduct, Vauxhall and Waterloo:
an almost interminable index of termini.

I love their noisiness: announcements, whistles;
trains arriving, trains departing;
the cheerful chatter of children, joy
of lovers meeting – the long silence
of lovers' separation; slammed doors, coffee-
machines, half-caught conversations;
the flap and flutter of frightened pigeons –
and anxious parents – iPlayers, ringtones:
a constant, comforting cacophony.

St. Pancras is a poet's station,
saved by a poet who opposed its demolition
in days when Victorian buildings were not valued as now:
John Betjeman, whose bronze statue
seems astonished by the single-span roof.
This railway cathedral offers routes to the Midlands;
Gatwick and Brighton, Bedford and Luton;
Brussels and Paris – and places beyond:
the magic of Eurostar, the romance of the railway.

TAVISTOCK SQUARE

I like to sit in London squares
to watch the pigeons, or the passers-by.
I know no better strategy to try
                to calm the soul, or soothe one's cares.

London's a chessboard: you can move
from square to square in search of quietness,
like pawns or pieces in a game of chess,
                until you feel your mood improve.

Study the statues. Watch the trees,
which never seem completely still – small birds
and breezes stir them. Nature transcends words
                to set the mind and heart at ease.

This is my favourite square of all,
where Eliot walked, and Gandhi talked of peace;
where those who hope and pray that wars may cease
                regard the cherry's blossom fall.

THE SENATE HOUSE

The University of London, later
by many centuries than Oxbridge is,
can justly claim to be that much the greater:
this mother of new universities
has long awarded external degrees
as both examiner and validator,
and was the Commonwealth's and colonies'
great nurse of learning, London's alma mater!

This is the Senate House, administrator
of a great academic empire. These
buildings contain a library, the data,
records, committee-rooms and offices
that form a modern university's
nerve-centre. Don't expect the elevator
to show the full extent of Bloomsbury's
great nurse of learning. London's alma mater!

This institution was the incubator
in which so many Schools and Colleges
grew to maturity, the mandator
of independent universities
across the nation – also overseas:
its offspring stretch from here to the equator.
It almost seems like half humanity's
great nurse of learning, London's alma mater!

Prince, pauper, all are welcome here: this is
a source of teaching and research, creator
of new and younger universities,
great nurse of learning, London's alma mater!

THE BRITISH MUSEUM

Founded by Sir Hans Sloane in 1753,
the British Museum acquired books and objects,
the Lindisfarne Gospels and the Lewis Chessmen,
the Franks Casket and the Cotton Library,
the Elgin Marbles and the manuscript of Beowulf –
until in 1997
the British Library with all its books and papers,
manuscripts and magazines,
migrated to a new site on the northern side
of the Euston Road.

      The Elgin Marbles
and the Rosetta Stone are striking examples
of disputed objects – artefacts claimed
by other nations, Egypt and Greece,
their countries of origin; others include
the Oxus Treasure from Tajikistan
and Ethiopian Tabots. Aboriginal
human remains have been handed back
to Australia already – the start of a programme
of restitution?

      This rich collection,
representing human history and artistry
from every age and every culture,
would still astonish the studious visitor,
if all that remained were English treasures,
the Franks Casket (Florence holds the right side:
perhaps they'd swap it for something Roman?),
the Mildenhall Hoard of marvellous silverware,
or the contents of the cemetery at Sutton Hoo,
a ship-burial of beautiful objects,
the greatest treasure in the entire collection.

SIR JOHN SOANE'S MUSEUM

Here is Dickens's London: lawyer-land –
the Inns of Court, Old Curiosity
Shop – with the Dickens Museum on hand.
But it's the Soane Museum, all agree,
that's most deserving of a visit (or
a verse) – if time (or space) won't let you see
(or me describe) a single marvel more.
Soane's home was here: he worked within (and on)
these three linked houses to create a store
of artefacts – which, after he was gone,
should go, not to his disinherited
son, George, but to the nation. Gaze upon
antiquities and sculptures: where you tread,
he trod two centuries ago, and made
this strange collection. Now, though he's long dead,
his spirit seems to haunt the place, his shade
yet animates his models and his drafts,
the mass of objects gained through gifts or trade,
devoted to the visual arts and crafts.
His architecture's part of what's on show:
the top-lit areas, permitting shafts
of light to fall upon the space below,
remind us of Soane's work at Dulwich and
the Bank. See it you must, before you go!

Covent Garden

This place, a replica of Paradise –
with sacred garden, fallen women, loss,
to parallel the Book of Genesis –
conceals more than it shows to those who cross
the Square today, intent on shopping. This
place has meant more than just pleasure – at a price!

A convent orchard first, before the king
destroyed the monasteries – and sent the nuns
to earn a living on the streets. The place
became a market-garden – orisons
displaced by street-cries, profit ousting grace;
the church and square built at another king's urging.

But soon the place fell into disrepute –
taverns and brothels, market-stalls and crime,
theatres and entertainment of the sort
where gentlemen might purchase a good time
with Betty Careless. Harlots could be bought
as easily (and cheap) as vegetables or fruit.

So Parliament decided to expel
the whores and make a covered market here.
It grew, attracting customers and loads
of produce: access routes were never clear.
Traffic of goods makes traffic on the roads.
One hell destroyed transforms into another hell.

The market was expelled in turn, and then
this 'tourist Covent Garden' came to be –
cafés, street-entertainment, shops and bars.
But fallen women aren't just history.
Hark! From the north-east tragic opera-stars
cry out in grief, 'Mia figlia!' – 'Mimi!' – 'Carmen!'

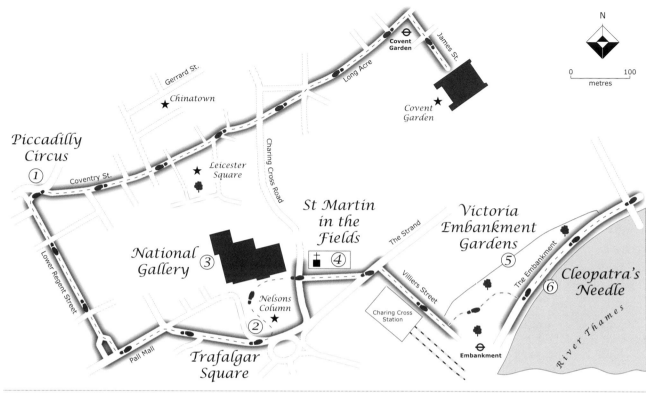

N

0 100
metres

Piccadilly Circus
①

Coventry St.

Gerrard St.

★ *Chinatown*

★ *Leicester Square*

Charing Cross Road

Long Acre

James St.

Covent Garden

★ *Covent Garden*

National Gallery ③

Lower Regent Street

St Martin in the Fields

† ■ ④

The Strand

Villiers Street

Victoria Embankment Gardens
⑤

The Embankment

Cleopatra's Needle
⑥

Nelsons Column

②

Charing Cross Station

Embankment

River Thames

Pall Mall

Trafalgar Square

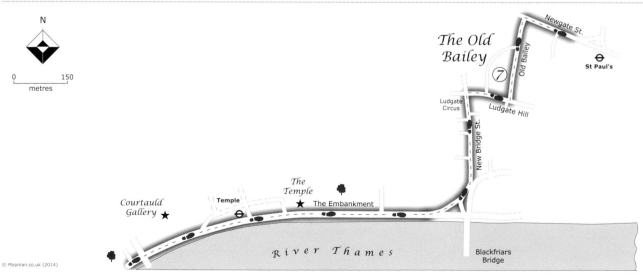

N

0 150
metres

The Old Bailey

Newgate St.

Old Bailey

⑦

St Paul's

Ludgate Circus

Ludgate Hill

New Bridge St.

Courtauld Gallery ★

Temple

The Temple

★ The Embankment

Blackfriars Bridge

River Thames

© Mapman.co.uk (2014)

4. THE HEART OF LONDON

THE FOURTH WALK STARTS AT COVENT GARDEN, where the previous one ended. Walk back up James Street and turn left into Long Acre. Continue south-westwards through Cranbourn Street, Leicester Square (with Chinatown on your right), and Coventry Street, to reach PICCADILLY CIRCUS.

Then walk southwards down Lower Regent Street and turn left when you come to Pall Mall, which brings you into TRAFALGAR SQUARE. The NATIONAL GALLERY is located on the north side of the Square; ST. MARTIN IN THE FIELDS lies to the east.

Now take Duncannon Street on the south side of the church, cross the Strand, and walk down Villiers Street to reach the VICTORIA EMBANKMENT GARDENS. CLEOPATRA'S NEEDLE is on the river-side of the Embankment a short distance to the north.

Continue north and east along the Embankment, admiring the river. You pass the Courtauld Gallery and The Temple to the left. When you reach Blackfriars Bridge, turn left up New Bridge Street, and then right at Ludgate Circus. You are on Ludgate Hill – and shortly turn left into Old Bailey, where you will find the Central Criminal Court – THE OLD BAILEY. Turn right into Newgate Street, where there are buses, and St. Paul's Tube Station at the far end.

PICCADILLY CIRCUS

The roundabout at Piccadilly, planned
by Holford (double-decked) was never made.
Instead, this Circus — where the tourists stand —
remains unaltered, much as when first laid
out by Nash: modest, functional, not grand ...

... nor altogether honest, I'm afraid.
The statue's Anteros, not Eros; and
the glory of the lights is much decayed.
(The sites reduce, as rental costs expand.)
A government by now should have re-planned
                              the roundabout.

Who's Anteros, you ask? The god displayed
is *charitable love*, mild, selfless, bland —
not passionate like love of man and maid.
Forget that tryst, your train, the traffic, trade:
study Lord Shaftesbury to understand
                              the roundabout.

TRAFALGAR SQUARE

Trafalgar Square's a place where common people
collect to celebrate, or protest. Lions
observe the scene unmoved, whilst lofty statues
calmly ignore the turmoil and the traffic
beneath their solemn gaze. A flock of pigeons
are picking at the scraps and drips from fountains

The fresh wind sprinkles water from the fountains
to fill the puddles and disturb the people.
An old man patiently is feeding pigeons;
a child is gazing   growling – at the lions;
and all around the ceaseless roar of traffic
offends the stillness of those mighty statues.

Study the names inscribed below the statues:
great English heroes, honoured by the fountains
adorning this great Square besieged by traffic,
those kings and famous leaders of the people,
generals and admirals who fought like lions,
the greatest, Nelson, with his crown of pigeons.

A modern Babel – languages and pigeons,
accents and dialects – surrounds the statues,
which wait with patient confidence, like lions,
for when, as England ruled the waves once (fountains
suggest the sea), the language of its people
shall mediate all global trade and traffic.

Beware the beggars, rogues and gangs who traffic
drugs; or pick tourists' pockets, like the pigeons
pecking a crust; or prey upon the people,
who lose their money while they look at statues,
their peace of mind as they admire those fountains
playing legato to the placid lions.

Trafalgar Square is famous – for its lions,
still guardians amidst the roaring traffic;
the sometimes empty plinth beside the fountains;
the Christmas Tree that comes from Norway; pigeons;
the victory it's named for; and those statues,
symbolic of the greatness of its people.

A place where lions seem to watch the traffic,
where fountains please the pigeons and the tourists,
while statues still inspire the English people.

THE NATIONAL GALLERY

Some of the very best of western culture's here:
The Martyrdom of Saint Sebastian
This Gallery is where these works of art appear.
Belshazzar's Feast; The Baptism of Christ
These priceless paintings here on public view
The Wilton Diptych; Snow at Argenteuil
Exemplify what visual art can do
The Adoration of the Golden Calf
To save the past, instruct, inspire and please
Equestrian Portrait of Charles the First
Those who come here to take their time and ease,
A portrait of the Duke of Wellington
Admiring form and colour, depth and line,
The Fighting Temeraire; Rain, Steam and Speed
Objects and figures, human and divine.
The Rokeby Venus; The Ambassadors

A picture's worth a thousand words, they say:
The Arnolfini Portrait; Whistlejacket
But what's the value of a work of art today?
The Hay Wain; Sunflowers; Les Parapluies
The skill and scarcity of what's on show
A Lady Seated at a Virginal
Is more than I may say, or we can know.
Portrait of Doge Leonardo Loredan
But the big question is: whether or not
Salome with the Head of John the Baptist
Art has a moral purpose? Or if what
Venus and Mars; The Death of Actaeon
You gaze at is just pretty decoration
Bathers at Asnières; Les Grandes Baigneuses
Collected here to entertain the nation?

St. Martin in the Fields

Built in the open fields between two cities –
Westminster, London, to the west and east –
devoted to the soldier-saint and priest,
Martin of Tours, this church is special: it is
renowned for music – and compassion. Pity's
as needful as is piety: the least –
the homeless and unloved – should share the feast.
Charity's acts of kindness, not committees!

So, say a prayer for Nell Gwynne, buried here.
Admire this parish church of Royalty,
designed by Gibbs. Attend a concert. Pause,
before you leave, to drop a gentle tear
for those in need, and share your charity.
This is a church of ever-open doors.

[87]

The Victoria Embankment Gardens

... extend from Blackfriars to Westminster Bridge
along the north side of the River Thames
on land reclaimed when Joseph Bazalgette
built his new sewer, ending the Great Stink –
a garden hiding one huge sewage pipe!
You wouldn't guess it now: the scent of flowers
replaces ordure's odours and the Thames,
once just an open sewer, harbours salmon.
Rest on a seat, and study all those statues:
John Tyndale, who began the English Bible;
Brunel, who engineered the western railways;
Sir Arthur Sullivan – 'the long day closes';
poets, philosophers, camels and soldiers.
Enjoy the concert – and a cup of tea.

CLEOPATRA'S NEEDLE

London is littered with the looted spoils
of England's cultural supremacy,
conquest and empire – a large fortune oils
the wheels of envy and cupidity.
Galleries and museums claim they own
those treasures taken from their rightful homes:
the Elgin Marbles or Rosetta Stone.
Should we return what's India's, what's Rome's?
This obelisk beside the Thames belongs
to Egypt and once rested near the Nile.
Perhaps time heals – but time does not right wrongs.
One day, not yet, the case must come to trial.
We can't repair old wounds of shot and sword,
but art and artefacts might be restored.

THE OLD BAILEY

Here Newgate Prison stood: now judges sit
at trials of major crimes in the Crown Court.
The law of wisdom is the fount of life.

Tradition grants the Lord Mayor pride of place:
the central chair is courteously left vacant –
for *London shall have all its ancient rights.*

This Court 'Defends the Children of the Poor,
and Punishes the Wrongdoer' – because
the welfare of the people is supreme.

The statue of Justitia appears
above the Court, with sword in hand, to show
right lives by law and law subsists by power.

Justice is blind, they say. Here Justice stands
unblinkered, unafraid, above the City
to *poise the cause in judgement's equal scales.*

The Parliament makes laws, and parliaments
are made by people's choices. Laws are sacred –
since *Moses gave the people laws from God.*

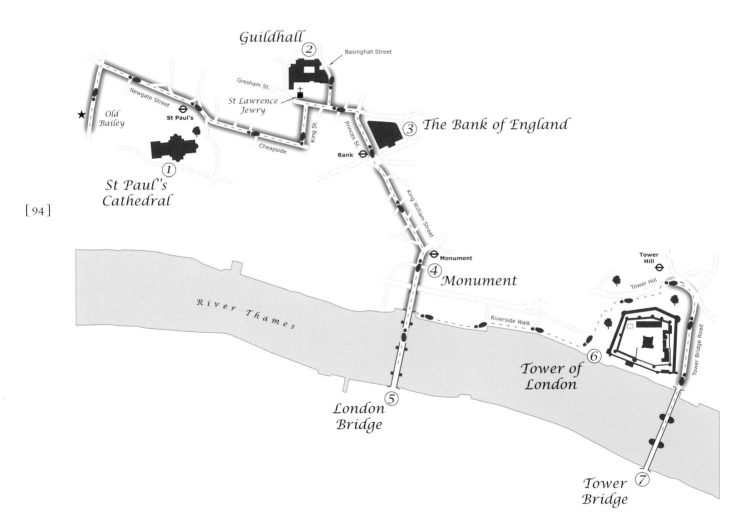

N

0 — 200
metres

Guildhall ②

Basinghall Street

Gresham St.

St Lawrence Jewry

Newgate Street

St Paul's

★ Old Bailey

Cheapside

King St.

Princes St.

Bank

③ The Bank of England

① St Paul's Cathedral

[94]

King William Street

Monument ④ **Monument**

River Thames

Riverside Walk

Tower Hill

Tower Hill

Tower Bridge Road

⑥ Tower of London

London Bridge ⑤

Tower Bridge ⑦

© Mapman.co.uk (2014)

5. THE CITY

THIS WALK BEGINS AT THE OLD BAILEY, where the previous one finished. Walk eastwards along Newgate Street to ST. PAUL'S CATHEDRAL, which is located just south of the tube station. Continue along Cheapside, but turn left (northwards) up King Street, leading to Gresham Street, where you will see St. Lawrence Jewry in front of GUILDHALL. Turn right and then left into Basinghall Street to find the entrance.

From there you should retrace your steps and continue eastwards along Gresham Street, turning right (south) down Princes Street to the Bank tube station and THE BANK OF ENGLAND. Continue southwards from here down King William Street to the Monument tube station. You will find THE MONUMENT itself at the west end of Monument Street.

Return to King William Street and turn left: walk out into the centre of LONDON BRIDGE. Enjoy the view. Then go back to the north bank of the river; follow the Thames Path sign to descend steps to the riverside. Turn left and follow the Riverside Walk to THE TOWER OF LONDON and TOWER BRIDGE.

ST. PAUL'S CATHEDRAL

A phoenix from the ashes – old St. Paul's
had perished in the Fire – Wren's masterpiece,
reborn and raised beside the Roman Walls!
(A building may revive, though we must cease.)
Both dominant and dignified, the dome –
a modern wonder of the world – remains
a London landmark. Greatness finds its home
within, though name and fame must fade, as wanes
the starlight, when the sun's first rays appear.
The modern buildings dwarf what once was tall –
as high in feet as days are in a year –
commanding London as the Church Saint Paul.
Resistless time transforms all things. Time must
reduce all lives, all monuments, to dust.

GUILDHALL

London's Guildhall once was a Roman sportsfield;
then became a centre for tax-collection;
but, before that, legend recounts that Brutus
                                    built a great palace ...

After Troy fell, those who survived dispersed all
over Europe: *Brutus* (it's said) ruled *Britain*.
Neither story nor derivation ring true.
                                    (Legends are legends.)

This Hall dates from 1411: London's
Great Fire burnt the roof, but the building survived –
and escaped again, when the Nazi fire-bombs
                                    made it their target.

Restorations altered and added features –
entrance, new roof – nothing remains completely
changeless – but this Guildhall is still the same great
                                    building it once was,

when the traitors (martyrs, perhaps?) were tried here –
Howard, Dudley, Cranmer and Lady Jane Grey ...
Study all those monuments: both Pitts, Nelson,
                                    Wellington, Churchill ...

Here, the new Lord Mayor of London's banquet
takes place. Here, Prime Ministers speak. Here, Chopin
played in his last public appearance. Feasting,
                                    speeches and music ...

Gog and Magog, giants that Brutus captured
are kept here. Their effigies (twice destroyed, and
twice replaced) are seen at the Lord Mayor's show: they
                                    lead the procession.

London's unique history is a patchwork –
fiction, half-truth, fact and tradition, muddled
up together, making a story you can't
                                    trust, but can treasure!

[99]

THE BANK OF ENGLAND

There are three *banks*: 'a ridge', 'a tier', 'a store
of money' – all derived from an old word
meaning 'a shelf'. Today, this transferred third
sense prevails: neither the Embankment, nor
a bank of oars, matters to London more
than England's ancient Central Bank (referred
to now as *The Old Lady* – an absurd
name from the ghost seen at the garden door.

Yet money is a spectre, value just
an apparition. Even England's gold
reserves are worth no more than markets say
they are. All banks can fail. The moth and rust
corrupt our treasures. *The Old Lady* may
make money, but banks, like banknotes, fold.

THE MONUMENT

Of all the columns in the world – of stone
this is the tallest one that stands alone:
the Monument to the Great Fire, which blazed
through London for three dreadful days, and razed
some 13,000 houses to the ground.
This slender fluted Doric column, crowned
with nothing but a gilded urn of fire,
is one of Wren's designs: it reaches higher
than sixty-seven yards – the distance to
where, in Pudding Lane, the fire started. You
should doubt the truth of the inscriptions. One
claims 'three short years' from when it was begun
the work of restoration was complete.
The Monument alone took twelve: conceit?
deceit? Another (now deleted) blamed
a 'Popish frenzy' for the storm which flamed
across the City. You should rather note
the verses of our English Pope, who wrote:
'Where London's column, pointing to the skies,
Like a tall bully, lifts the head, and lies.'

LONDON BRIDGE

The silent river flows towards the sea,
And twice each day the swelling tides return.
Stand in the centre of the bridge and learn
The littleness of human history.
The silent river flows towards the sea,
And twice each day the swelling tides return.
Look north – the City – where the have-lots earn
Still more wealth in their money-factory.
The silent river flows towards the sea,
And twice each day the swelling tides return.
Look south – the suburbs – where the have-nots burn
With envy at such gross cupidity.
The silent river flows towards the sea,
And twice each day the swelling tides return.
Look west to where these waters rise: they yearn
To join the sullen, sempiternal sea.
The silent river flows towards the sea,
And twice each day the swelling tides return.
Look east at last towards the dawn, and learn
To face the truth that we must cease to be.
The silent river flows towards the sea,
And twice each day the swelling tides return.

THE TOWER OF LONDON

The Tower of London's where they keep the Jewels
that form the royal regalia: a castle
built by the Conqueror, where Yeoman Warders,
the Royal Bodyguard, maintained a prison
fit for the monarch's enemies and traitors,
great Tudor Queens, young Princes, ghosts – and lions.

The Royal Menagerie, with bears and lions
and elephants, was here – and the Crown Jewels
still are – and here in two World Wars our traitors
and spies were executed. This great castle,
a palace once for kings and queens, a prison
later, is now where ravens live with Warders.

The Beefeaters, the Tower's Yeoman Warders,
in Tudor costume, who controlled the lions,
now care for ravens: once, guards in a prison,
today they're guides – show tourists the Crown Jewels
and pose for pictures in this ancient castle,
while telling stories of the ghosts of traitors.

The Tower is where they used the rack; where traitors
faced death by axe or bullet – grim rewarders
of treachery – where this great Norman castle
has made a home for monarchs – and for lions –
the Royal Mint and Treasure (the Crown Jewels
remain). But, most of all, it's been a prison.

Guy Fawkes was tortured here; and in this prison
Ann Boleyn died, and Hess was held. The Traitors'
Gate welcomed great ones to their fate – the jewels
of history. Wyatt, Raleigh, More ... The Warders
survive, protecting ravens – which, like lions,
protect England – until they leave the castle.

Admire the White Tower of William's castle.
Imagine those who suffered in this prison,
the Lady Jane Grey – elephants and lions –
unlucky losers or misguided traitors
(all guarded by these faithful Yeoman Warders)
and Colonel Blood, who tried to steal the Jewels.

The Tower was a castle and a prison
where lions gambolled once, and traitors died,
and Warders guard the Crown Jewels today.

TOWER BRIDGE

Rising to let the tall ships past,
This bridge, the first the sailor sees,
Coming to London, and the last,
Before he meets the North Sea breeze –

This bridge, the first the sailor sees:
The last, proceeding down the Thames,
Before he meets the North Sea breeze
And loses sight of London's gems –

The last, proceeding down the Thames,
He passes, as he leaves the City
And loses sight of London's gems,
The bridge is striking, if not pretty!

He passes, as he leaves the City,
This bridge of towers we call Tower Bridge:
The bridge is striking, if not pretty –
But finding fault is sacrilege!

This bridge of towers we call Tower Bridge,
The strangest sight of all to see
(But finding fault is sacrilege)
That lingers in the memory.

The strangest sight of all to see,
Coming to London, and the last
That lingers in the memory,
Rising to let the tall ships past.

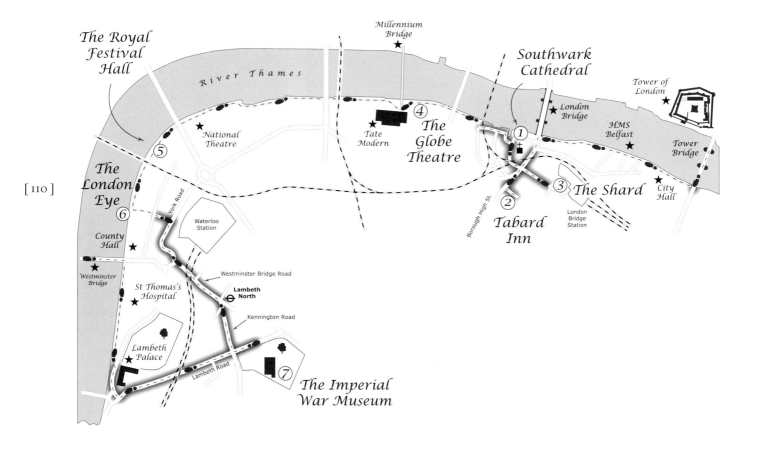

N

0 ———— 250
metres

The Royal
Festival
Hall

River Thames

Millennium
Bridge ★

Southwark
Cathedral

Tower of
London ★

★ National
Theatre

Tate
Modern ★ ■

④ The
Globe
Theatre

① ★ London
Bridge

HMS
Belfast ★

Tower
Bridge

⑤

The
London
Eye

⑥

York Road

Waterloo
Station

Borough High St.

②
③ The Shard

London
Bridge
Station

City
Hall ★

County
Hall ★

Tabard
Inn

★ Westminster
Bridge

St Thomas's
Hospital ★

Westminster Bridge Road

Lambeth
North

Kennington Road

Lambeth
Palace ★

Lambeth Road

⑦

The Imperial
War Museum

6. THE SOUTH BANK

THIS WALK STARTS AT THE SOUTHERN END OF TOWER BRIDGE and, apart from a few detours, takes you back along the south bank of the Thames to Westminster Bridge. Walking westwards, you pass HMS Belfast on the right, and City Hall and London Bridge Station, where you can find the London Dungeon, on your left.

When you reach London Bridge, turn left into Borough High Street to find SOUTHWARK CATHEDRAL (on the right) and the site of Chaucer's TABARD INN – further along on the left.

Return towards the river, but then turn right up London Bridge Street to reach THE SHARD. Go back to the river and continue along the towpath westwards to find THE GLOBE THEATRE.

Continue westwards past the Millennium Bridge and Tate Modern – and, further on, the National Theatre. As the river bends towards the south, you come to THE ROYAL FESTIVAL HALL.

Continue beneath the railway bridge leading to Charing Cross Station on the opposite bank: THE LONDON EYE is ahead of you.

Now, with Westminster Bridge in sight beyond County Hall, turn left into Chichely Street, then right into York Road and left again into Westminster Bridge Road. Branch right at Lambeth North tube station into Kennington Road. Turn left into Lambeth Road, where you will find the entrance to THE IMPERIAL WAR MUSEUM on the right.

Return to the river along Lambeth Road. When you reach Lambeth Bridge, turn northwards along the tow-path. You pass Lambeth Palace and St. Thomas's Hospital, before you finally come to Westminster Bridge and complete our long circular tour of London.

SOUTHWARK CATHEDRAL

A place of compromise and contradictions –
ancient and modern, actual and fanciful:
a nunnery founded by a ferryman's daughter
(her name was Mary)   then a monastery dedicated
to the Virgin Mary, Mother of the Saviour.
Perhaps ... perhaps not; history or legend?
After the Conquest an Austin Priory
was certainly here, sacred to St. Mary
Overie – which means 'over the water'.
After the Dissolution, rededicated to her Son,
the Priory became the parish church
of St. Saviour, a Southwark landmark –
but not a cathedral until 1905.
This building is now sacred to both the Son and his Mother.
Study the monuments and memorials within:
Nelson Mandela and Desmond Tutu;
great benefactors and forgotten bishops;
the painted tomb of the poet, Gower;
England's history of heretics and playwrights,
ruination and reconstruction,
fresh adventures and the vice of nostalgia,
established facts and fanciful traditions,
common sense and sentimentality –
each one is celebrated in Southwark's Cathedral.

The Tabard Inn

Six hundred years ago, and more, a famous poet
named Geoffrey Chaucer wrote a story-book: we know it
still as *The Canterbury Tales*. It started here,
where once there used to be a pilgrims' inn quite near.
In fact, there was a good deal more than one such inn:
the poet mentions one 'close by', The Bell, and in
the neighbourhood a later writer lists The Spur,
The George, a Queen's Head and a King's Head – and there were
others which catered for the pilgrims on the way
to Canterbury. This is what Chaucer has to say:

When April comes, bringing its soothing showers
After a dry March to infuse the flowers
With rain, which swells the slender shoots, and floods
All plants with juice to feed those breaking buds;
And when soft winds and gentle airs inspire
The farmer's tender seedlings in each shire;
And the spring sun is halfway down the track
Of lusty Aries in the Zodiac;
And the small birds sing madrigals all day
(They sleep at night with open eyes, they say!)
As nature prompts, in fields and foliage;
Then people yearn to make a pilgrimage
And travellers to see some strange new place,
Or distant shrines, made sacred by God's grace;
And, most of all, from every shire and see
In England, off they go to Canterbury

To find that blest and holy martyr, who
Helped them when they were feeling sick, or blue.
And so it was that at that time, one day,
In Southwark at the Tabard Inn (I stay
There while I get myself prepared to start
My trip to Canterbury with a good heart)
There came that night into the hostelry
Some twenty-nine souls in a company
Of diverse folk who'd met by chance – a band
Of pilgrims from all corners of the land –
Who wished to take the road to Canterbury.
The rooms were good; the stables seemed to be
Ample; and we were welcomed by
Our Host. And when the sun sank from the sky
I'd got to know the company so well
That I'd become a member too, to tell
The truth. We all agreed not to be late
For the excursion, which I now relate .....

[115]

But that was then, and this is now. Six centuries
have passed, and Harry Bailly's famous hostelry's
no more. The Tabard was destroyed by fire; restored,
renamed The Talbot, to provide warm bed and board
for stage-coach passengers – before the railway age,
which cut the effort (and reward) of pilgrimage,
made it redundant, and it was demolished. Look
at the blue plaque – or, better still, read Chaucer's book.

THE SHARD

Some buildings challenge us:
the Shard is one.
Briefly the tallest building
in the whole of Europe,
English Heritage was un-persuaded
by the plans –
and in a droll critique
claimed it would be
'a shard of glass piercing the heart of London'.
That Great Heart has suffered worse!
Approved as a first-class design,
the Shard's a triumph
of the art of architecture
and construction skills.
One thousand feet in height,
its glass and steel
offer climbers – abseilers – jumpers – thrills;
and challenge us
to credit what we feel:
the constant wonder
of emergent form –
like sunlight piercing rainclouds in a storm.

THE GLOBE THEATRE

'The cloud-capped towers, the gorgeous palaces
The solemn temples, the great globe itself ...'
(Shakespeare, *The Tempest*)

Is London just an insubstantial pageant,
fading like dreams or dramas on the stage?
Will was a poet too – another sad gent
wrestling with rhymes and words to earn a living wage.

He wrote his plays for this great London theatre:
Hamlet, The Henrys, Much Ado, The Dream ...
where tragedy and comedy appear to
be realler than our real lives may sometimes seem.

No citizen has ever served this City
better; none has deserved more gratitude.
Honour his name; applaud his plays; but pity
all planets of a star of so great magnitude.

THE ROYAL FESTIVAL HALL

Built on a brewery site for the Festival,
opened in May, 1951 – modernist,
'egg-in-a-box' design – altered and added to
several times in the decades that followed – just
recently given a major refurbishment –
this is a Festival Hall with a difference –
foyers providing the public with popular
rendezvous – you can find rest and refreshment here –
concerts of classical music and dance attract
thousands to this Grade 1 Listed construction –
beautiful? hardly! – but certainly striking – it's
well worth a visit for coffee (and overtures?)
music and biscuits, a beer or a symphony.

The London Eye

The London I delight to know
requires a careful choice of view:
bridges across the river show
the City at its best, for who
does not admire the subtle glow
water gives buildings? Very few
of those who walk in London do
learn to look closer, or grow
                  the 'London eye'
which spots its secret charms. Or go
to some high vantage-point where you
may see the City's sights below –
from Hampstead Heath, the Shard, or through
                  the London Eye.

THE IMPERIAL WAR MUSEUM

Originally a hospital
for the insane, this place is full
of guns and tanks, war-planes and warships. War,
which pacifists deplore (and most ignore),
is celebrated here,
it seems, while warfare's sheer
insanity – which should disgust
us all – is not. Is this place just
a monument to military glory,
parts best forgotten of our island's story?

The suicidal madness of
civilisation: Molotov
cocktails, grenades, machine-guns, atom bombs,
gas, total war, the Holocaust, pogroms ...
Here, visitors explore
the striking arts of war,
film, photographs, and paintings. These
reveal the grim realities
of modern war, the pity and the price –
that proud *record of toil and sacrifice.*

The history of modern war
is what this great Museum's for:
war-study and war's understanding is
the duty of all free democracies,
like ours. One hundred years
of conflict, courage, tears –
of triumph and disaster – are
recorded here from battles far
and near, fought in the skies, on land and sea:
one long campaign to set all nations free.

[125]

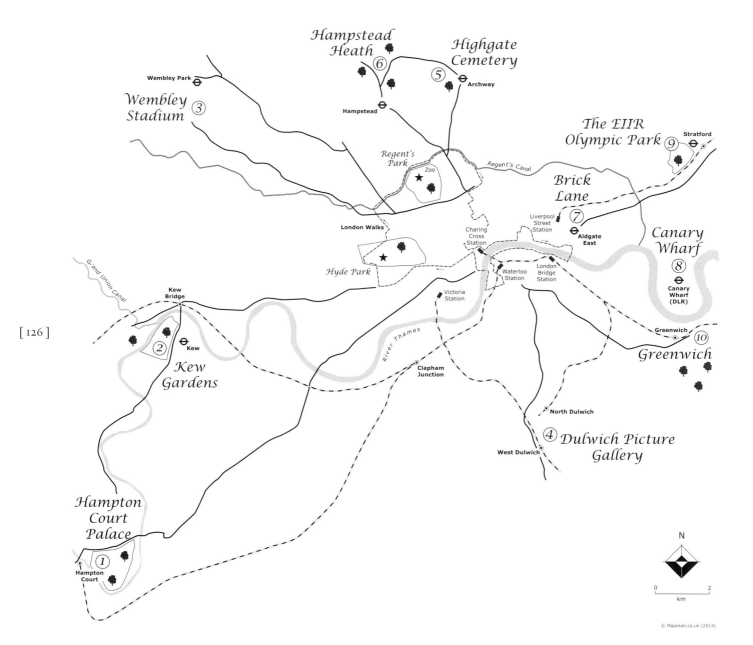

Hampstead
Heath
⑥

Highgate
Cemetery
⑤

Wembley Park ⊖

Wembley
Stadium ③

Archway

Hampstead

The EIIR
Olympic Park ⑨

Stratford

Regent's
Park
Zoo ★

Regent's Canal

Brick
Lane
⑦

Liverpool
Street
Station

Aldgate
East

Canary
Wharf
⑧

London Walks

Charing
Cross
Station

Hyde Park ★

Waterloo
Station

London
Bridge
Station

Canary
Wharf
(DLR)

Grand Union Canal

Kew
Bridge

②

Kew

Kew
Gardens

Victoria
Station

River Thames

Clapham
Junction

Greenwich

Greenwich ⑩

North Dulwich

④ Dulwich Picture
Gallery

West Dulwich

Hampton
Court
Palace

①

Hampton
Court

N

0 ———— 2
km

© Mapman.co.uk (2014)

[126]

7. SOME SIGHTS AROUND LONDON

WE HAVE CHOSEN ten sights dotted around the periphery of central London. Some can be reached on foot, by walking westwards (upstream) along the river – KEW GARDENS, and rather further, HAMPTON COURT PALACE – or eastwards (downstream) GREENWICH.

Others, like BRICK LANE, CANARY WHARF or THE EIIR OLYMPIC PARK, are not far from the east end of the City.

THE DULWICH PICURE GALLERY is in south London. You can reach it by train from Victoria Station.

The remainder are in north London, accessible by tube train or bus: WEMLEY STADIUM, HIGHGATE CEMETERY and HAMPSTEAD HEATH. We hope that the map will help you find your way to these outlying sights.

HAMPTON COURT PALACE

– is haunted by the ghosts of queens and kings:
Jane Seymour, Catherine Howard, and their spouse –
King Henry – each are seen around the house;
while Sybil Pen, who died of smallpox, brings
her spinning-wheel to life again. Such things
defy belief. But Wolsey's presence is
still felt within this place, which once was his.

He built it – and then gave it to the King.
The Cardinal, who fell from royal grace
and favour, could not save himself. Disgrace
can't be bought off – and those who try to cling
to power, once it's lost, are little more
than fading spirits, waiting at death's door.

This Palace is a composite of styles:
Domestic Tudor, Perpendicular
Gothic, Italian Renaissance, here are
astonishingly harmonised. These piles
of pink brick and pale Portland stone bring smiles
of admiration to discerning eyes –
a miracle of English compromise.

But architecture also has its ghosts:
Wren's Palace, with its dome, was not to be.
Baroque Versailles lacks English modesty.
For all its dignity, this Palace boasts
a kind of reticence – as gracious hosts,
who seek to please the honoured guest,
will treat her well, not seek to be the best.

Queen Mary Tudor's phantom pregnancy
persisted here: she died without an heir.
Imprisoned here, before he had to bare
his neck to meet the axe, King Charles must be
a headless ghost today – for those who see
such apparitions. Thrown from horseback here,
King William met his death within a year.

Visit the gardens, maze, the great grapevine
(the largest in the world), Wren's Lion Gate,
the Great Hall and the Chapel Royal. Wait
to view the Clock, with astrologic sign,
tide, time, date, moon, the month and year, beside
Anne Boleyn's Gate – another queen who died

before her time – another queen who felt
the axe upon her neck. Another ghost.
So many ghosts are here! The Monarch's most
esteemed retainers, those who served and knelt
in loyalty, and then retired, have dwelt
at Hampton Court in recent years. Their faith's
rewarded in this house of royal wraiths.

Yet not since George II has a king
or queen chosen to make their residence
within this Palace. Visitors may sense
the presence of the past, the ghosts who cling
to royalty, but not the real thing.
This place, embodying what history means,
is haunted by those ghosts of kings and queens.

KEW GARDENS

Here is a paradise to please a gardener!
An ample arboretum – and an alphabet of species:
alpines, azaleas, arums and ferns;
bamboos, berberis, bonsai and grasses;
carnivores, cacti, aquatics and roses ...
Visit Kew Palace, the Palm House and Pagoda;
the Temperate House and Treetop Walkway.
Linger at the compost-heap – the largest in Europe!
But where on earth is the apple-tree?

The apple-tree is the Tree of Knowledge –
of right and wrong, reason and superstition,
good and evil, in the garden of life –
and the life of gardens. The library, museum,
seed-bank, herbarium, laboratory and plant-list,
each house a hoard of horticultural
and botanic knowledge – natural science,
botanical medicine, and the nomenclature of plants.
So, where on earth is the apple-tree?

You might buy an apple in the Orangery Restaurant,
and eat it on the train that tours the garden;
then search the conservatories, the Sackler Crossing;
the Order Beds and the orchid collection;
botanical art in each of the galleries;
the Japanese House or the juniper collection –
combing the gardens at Kew, like Adam
in Paradise, before you finally discover –
just where on earth is the apple-tree.

Wembley Stadium

The Wembley Arch replaces the two towers
of the old National Stadium here.
New Wembley – mobile roof, and tier on tier
of seats for 90,000 – offers hours
of football to the fans. This game of ours
(beautiful game!) we gave away. I fear
we may be waiting decades for the year
our soccer makes us one of the world-powers.

[132]   It also offers a case study in
project management – cost-overrun,
delays, and litigation about whose
fault it was ... Never mind! If England win,
a day at Wembley can be lots of fun:
and if they lose – at least there's lots of loos,

more than in any other stadium
around the globe! What else is special here:
the Lottery's (unused) athletics track;
the pitch – relaid a dozen times! – and some
of the great goals great players strike, or steer
into the net, to crown a swift attack.

And other forms of football can be found
at Wembley: gridiron, Rugby Union,
and Rugby League. The stadium is one
of the most popular venues around
the Capital for concerts: in this ground
George Michael and Madonna played – but none
more moving than the crowd, in unison,
singing 'Abide with me' – a solemn sound.

DULWICH PICTURE GALLERY

The arts conspire. One actor, Edward Alleyn,
founded the College – and another, Kemble,
persuaded Francis Bourgeois and his partner
to found, and build, and fill this Gallery with
the pictures they'd collected across Europe.
(Their bones are buried in the Mausoleum.)
The oldest public gallery in England
opened its doors two hundred years ago to
visitors – who included Etty, Turner,
Vincent van Gogh, and Constable. Charles Dickens
mentioned the Gallery in *Pickwick Papers*.
John Soane's design taught other architects the
way to display great art in natural light.
The arts conspire for public benefit.
The Gallery attracted thieves – and donors,
like Linley, Beechey, Murray, who gave paintings:
Rembrandt's small portrait of Jacob de Gheyn has
been stolen (and recovered) four times, setting
a world record for purloined art! Great artists,
with pictures on display, include Van Dyke, Cuyp,
Gainsborough, Poussin, Raphael, Reynolds, Rubens ...
Old Masters, the Baroque, and British Portraits –
despite the bomb which hit the Mausoleum,
scattering bones across the lawn – create here
one of the nation's finest art collections:
the Dulwich Picture Gallery – itself, too,
a noble work of art. *The arts conspire.*

[135]

HIGHGATE CEMETERY

The past's beyond our reach to change or cure.
This present's all there is, for life is here;
and what's to come (save death) is still obscure.

These names, but not those named here, still endure.
They lived, and died. And may not reappear.
The past's beyond our reach to change or cure.

This cemetery, with all its strange allure,
instructs the visitor: what is, is clear –
and what's to come (save death) is still obscure.

Nature revives a graveyard, that's for sure:
sad eyes, these trees may please, these flowers cheer.
The past's beyond our reach to change or cure.

Here's a memento mori. Tombs immure
the dead, reminding us our end is near,
and what's to come (save death) is still obscure.

Only this present moment is secure.
We may not live to see another year.
The past's beyond our reach to change or cure,
and what's to come (save death) is still obscure.

HAMPSTEAD HEATH

The Heath provides a playground for the people
of London: parkland, woods, the ponds and hills,
where you can see the domes and towers and steeples
spread out below, like toys on windowsills.

The Heath is common land, available
to all – to walk, or swim, play games, or fly
a kite. Some run. Some linger by the pool.
Some sit alone and watch the world go by.

The Heath is home to wildlife: slow-worms, frogs,
rabbits and foxes, squirrels, grass-snakes, deer –
living in constant fear of walkers' dogs.
Bats, parakeets and kingfishers are here.

They say the Heath's where Boadicea, the Queen
of the Iceni, lies interred. (Maybe.)
A windmill, once, turned its great sails where green
grass grows today. There's nothing left to see.

The Heath's encompassed by delights: Kenwood
(concerts), Golders Hill Park (which has a zoo),
and Parliament Hill Fields. The tourist should
climb Kite Hill – and then marvel at the view.

BRICK LANE

Here is a story of diversity and change.
Brick Lane was formerly known as Whitechapel Lane.
Famous for bricks and brewing, weaving, market-stalls
(and Sunday markets), food and fashion, modern art
(graffiti) – what, I wonder, will it offer next?
Social variety improves communities.

Here's a kaleidoscope: the picture changes as
the people change. New waves of immigrants displace
the earlier settlers: first, the Huguenots from France,
then Irish labourers, then Jews. Now 'Banglatown'
is home to Bangladeshis from Bengal, and claims
to be the curry capital of the UK.

Here is a chapel which, in turn, has served the French,
the missionaries, the Methodists – and then became
a synagogue – and now is the Great London Mosque,
which teaches the Five Practices of Islam. They
provide a discipline of life that all might learn:
study, pray, fast, give alms, and make a pilgrimage.

Here is a street which offers hope to all the world;
where diverse cultures, different colours, coexist
in peace, and make a virtue of variety.
Here's a place where the people seem to welcome change.
They change the language and the culture as they learn
new ways. In Brick Lane nothing ever stays the same.

CANARY WHARF

London's a city of circles and curves,
of roundabouts and river-bends,
circuses and crescents, of clocks and wheels:
Olympic rings, the London Eye,
the Circle Line, Belisha Beacons
or those Boris bikes for busy commuters –
and the economic cycles at Canary Wharf.

Canary Wharf is where money's made
(and lost) in minutes – and in millions. Finance
now finds its home here, beyond the City,
where the West India Docks on the Isle of Dogs
once liked to boast this was the busiest seaport
in the whole world. High-rise buildings
crowd together in Canada Square.

Canada Square is the centre and origin
of all this growth and wealth. A web of transport –
roads and railways, river and aircraft,
towpath and bus-routes, tube trains at the stations
on the Docklands Light Railway and the Jubilee Line extension
(together with Crossrail to come) – connects
this rich district to the rest of the Capital.

Capital is the reward for work, or investment –
buy low, sell high: work hard, work smart.
Short trade cycles turn like the seasons,
regularly enriching or ruining investors
who read them right – or wrong. (The first
developers went bankrupt!) But Kondratiev
saw another, longer, cycle – which may yet sink London ...

[143]

THE EIIR OLYMPIC PARK

Look back towards that great Olympic year –
the ceremonies, medals ... legacy:
look forward to this Royal Park to be,
named for the Queen, the nation's souvenir
of sporting glory ... there were heroes here.
And we are promised plenty more to see:
rich programmes of athletic poetry
of motion viewers may admire and cheer.

But sporting spectacle is but a part
of what is planned to please posterity –
a new museum of Olympic sport,
new university where sport is taught,
gardens and wetlands, a great work of art,
and homes – to form a new community.

GREENWICH

Like flies in amber, we are locked in time.
Our island is encompassed by the sea.
Greenwich provides the home and history
of seafaring, the origin and prime
marker of latitude and measurement
of time; teaches what Mean Time means – and meant

to sailors. Here's the oldest Royal Park,
Royal Observatory, the Museum,
the Queen's House: each explains why tourists come
to Greenwich. Don't forget the Cutty Sark,
the last of the great ships that brought us tea
from China. And there's even more to see.

Visit the Market, and the famous inn,
Trafalgar Tavern, by the river, and
the Royal Naval College, which was planned
by Wren, replacing an old palace, in
which were born two Tudor Queens and King
Henry, their father, during England's spring.

England today's autumnal. It's the fall
of a long year of enterprise and glory.
People come here to read that splendid story
of past achievements. Query: is that all
we have to offer now? Not quite. Stand on
the starting line of London's Marathon.

ENVOI

A man who's tired of London's tired of life,
said Doctor Johnson.   And that's also true,
today, for all of us: child, husband, wife;
tourist and resident; the reader – you;
the artist and the publisher and poet.
No matter how we seek to learn all London's
secrets to reach its mighty heart, and know it
fully, we'll not exhaust its rich abundance.
We'll always find here, hosts and guests alike,
more sights that please, surprise and entertain.
Reader, we hope you will – like us, and like
Dick Whittington – return again, again
explore each corner of this city's wards,
for London offers all that life affords.

ACKNOWLEDGEMENTS

The authors and publishers would like to acknowledge
the assistance of the following in the creation
of the paintings in this book:

Painting of Southwark Cathedral re-produced by kind
permission of The Chapter of Southwark Cathedral;
painting of Brompton Oratory with permission of the
Fathers of the Oratory, London; permission to draw
inside the museum by courtesy of the Trustees of Sir
John Soane's Museum.